Eric Moutsos wades into the modern  and provides an independent, unflinching insider's account of the pressures the front-line police officer faces while serving their communities. Ticket quotas, long a jealously guarded secret of chiefs, mayors, and city judges, are put in the spotlight, and the powers-that-be are exposed for their unethical practices- for which the men and women on the street pay the price. The story of the American cop matters- and readers wanting to understand what life on the street is really like for the heroes of American law enforcement will come away from Eric's story under-standing why.

Ian Adams
Executive Director
Utah Fraternal Order of Police

"Moutsos is not just a good cop and good man, he's a good storyteller. Every American who cares about freedom and fairness should read this book. Government officials abused their power, broke the law and a compliant media lets them get away with it."

Maggie Gallagher

"This book is the tip of the iceberg of what is to come."
Mike Hardin (Retired 20 year veteran Salt Lake City Police)

"Full of unexpected twists and turns, and the boyish excitement with which you tell it keeps me turning the pages in anticipation of the next big adventure. What I love most is the thread of faith and family that runs through it all."
Natalie Robison

"Eric's story is heart wrenching and eye opening. It is terrifying that this quotaism, as Eric calls it, is such a rampant problem. I commend him for having the courage to share his story. Something needs to change."
-**Nichelle Aiden**

DISPATCHED
CONSCIENCE OR CONFORMITY

by

Eric Moutsos

"Never do anything against conscience

even if the state demands it."

Albert Einstein

This is based on a true story and the retelling of actual events are not verbatim in some of the conversations you will read. The names of locations and people have been changed to protect the innocent . . . and the guilty.

Warning:

Reader discretion is advised in a few chapters that address suicide, pornography addiction, drug and alcohol abuse, and other violent police scenes that may not be recommended for children or sensitive readers.

For the American Cop and the Communities that We Serve

FOREWORD

This story matters.

We are at a time when public scrutiny of law enforcement has never been higher. We are at a time when any given police action is apt to be digitized, shared, dissected, and devoured endlessly on the internet. No one knows this better than former Salt Lake City Police Officer Eric Moutsos. In 2014, his story sprang to the front pages of local media. It spread to national news. It reached international media, too.

I met Eric shortly after his superiors placed him on administrative leave, seizing his badge for the purported sin of discrimination. The Salt Lake City Police Department leaked a misleading narrative to the media, breaking their own policies in the process. Their purpose seems to have been twofold: to simultaneously cover up a sexual harassment scandal within the office, and to embarrass and crush then Officer Eric Moutsos, thereby making him an example to other officers: sit down and shut up; obey without hesitation; conform and disregard conscience.

Many wanted him to sit still, to remain silent, and the Eric Moutsos I first encountered was happy to oblige.

He was frozen by fear and uncertainty. But then came the thaw and, with it, the courage to speak the truth. His story is an opportunity to show our community and this Nation (if not the global media who covered him) what it really means to be a cop in America today, while exposing some very real problems in law enforcement.

This story magnifies the reality that "problem policing" is more a byproduct of the machine of law enforcement than it is of any one officer, good or bad. By focusing on one breaking news story at a time, on one officer at a time, we lose sight of the devices that create and foster the type of policing that offends and divides. More importantly, by blaming and devouring the officers offered up by the machine, we forget that it is the machine that needs repair. We cannot make positive changes to law enforcement in the dark. We cannot make improvements if we talk about the wrong issues. This memoir will help you, the reader, understand the real wedge being driven between law enforcement and the community.

Only by investigating the true underlying mechanisms in the machine of law enforcement will we be able to break the faulty system and forge something better in its place.

I am grateful for this story, and that my friend has the heart to tell it to you. I hope it helps you view his story and other stories about law enforcement in a new light.

It has been my absolute privilege to know Eric, and it is without hesitation that I recommend his memoir, regardless of your take on cops, city politics, modern controversies of religious and individual rights, the US Constitution, or our Republic form of government. Read this memoir; tell somebody else to read it. My hope is that it starts a real discussion. I hope that conversation will remind us of our conscience and create change.

Stay Safe,

Bret W. Rawson

General Counsel, Utah State Lodge

Fraternal Order of Police

To the reader,

I am not a victim.

Throughout my career I made many mistakes and fell into many pitfalls because of my own pride and ignorance. There were many battles I shouldn't have fought, and many battles I should have.

There were times I stayed silent when I should have spoke, and many times when my voice brought consequences you'll now read about. But with every choice, as you'll see, there is a consequence good or bad. This is a good thing in the end, even when bad things happen. This is how we learn. Looking back, I truly can't believe I made it seven years in Law Enforcement. That alone was a miracle for a reason.

I also did things that have resulted in helping several internal police policies change in Salt Lake City, along with two laws change on the books in Utah. So with this said, I wouldn't change a thing. It was worth it. Because there needed to be change in some of these areas.

With the pressures from political police administrations and the public, the American Police Officer is sandwiched between. And the thin blue line continues to get thinner each day. We need cops. We need good cops. And we need those good cops to become the next leaders or the relationship between the police and the public will only get worse. It's the only way. Yes, the system is broken in many areas, but does that mean we give up and watch it happen in front of us?

One of my messages in the book is how to overcome adversity in the darkest hours. If we let it, that opposition will teach, sharpen and refine each one of us. Opposition is what can make us rock solid in our convictions.

For years I had some lingering poison in my veins for what happened to me and my family, I have played the victim game, and I still catch a trace of it here and there within, but today, overall I am so grateful for what happened.

I'm thankful to my old Chief of Police for taking my badge and my gun. I'm thankful for some of my Sergeants that sat silent, and for my Lieutenant who looked away when I stared at him for help. I know that sounds crazy, but I am.

The opposition helped force me to stay on my knees in prayer a whole lot longer than normal. The opposition helped me find God on a deeper level. The opposition helped me have no other option than to find a lot better version of myself. The opposition helped me find confidence in myself, and ironically, has allowed me to use my voice even more for what I believe.

And for the few who were with us, we will be friends forever and I'll never forget you. Thank you.

I hope my stories will inspire you to listen to your conscience and act, especially when you don't want to act. To face your fears. To not be afraid to use your voice and influence wherever you may be. Whatever that belief is. Because it matters. Your voice and passions do matter. It's why the Founders of our country did what they did, for you to speak and be a positive force for good.

And last, I hope this will ultimately help bring people together through our inevitable disagreements on sometimes polarizing topics. It is possible to love and disagree all at the same time; it's vital we do it. It means we aren't lying to each other. That's honest love.

Sincerely,

Eric Moutsos

Acknowledgements -

Besides **God** at the helm, I want to thank amazing and beautiful wife **Stacey**. She is my everything. My 4 incredible children who keep me moving every day, Ava, Devery, Chris and Rachel. Sherri Moutsos (Mom) Nick Moutsos (Dad), In-laws, Ed and Bobbie Carroll. My siblings, Casey and Brad Pace, Dustin and Mindy Moutsos, Ashley and Tyler Bell and their families.Evander Holyfield,, D.E, Kathy Smith, Joe Kerry, Paul Mero, Laurie and Stan Swim, Mike Erickson, Jack Phillips, David Christensen, Stephen Mongie, Scott and Barbara Morath, Evan Bush, Eric Marsing, Cody Gray, Michael Barber, Mick Fredericks, Rod Arquette, Adam Nicolaysen, Chris Nielsen, Tyler Austin, Bill Manzanares, Ammon Mauga, Bob Eldard, Andy Jackson, Mark Schuman, Jeremy Forman, Anthony Lane, Robert and Trish, Peggy Tidwell, Spencer Robinson, Ian Adams, Nate Nelson, Jeremy Jones.

A special thanks to Brian Goeckeritz for helping me shape, write, and articulate this book in ways I could have never been able to on my own. And for his sweet wife, Nicole, for the countless hours Brian was away from you to help me.

Bret Rawson (Legal) Stephanie Clayburn (Editor) Abraham Corona (Book cover graphics) Randy Anglesey (Photos for cover from Studio Defy) and Mike A. (Webpage).

CHAPTER 1

Just the Beginning

"Our culture has accepted two huge lies. The first is that if you disagree with someone's lifestyle, you must fear or hate them. The second is that to love someone means you agree with everything they believe or do. Both are nonsense. You don't have to compromise convictions to be compassionate."

Rick Warren

The morning and early afternoon of June 4, 2014, felt different from any other day that I'd gone to work in my seven years as an officer for the Salt Lake City Police Department. A sense of dread shrouded my thoughts. My gut warned me, seemed to whisper, *"Hey, Eric, pay attention. Something is not right."* My experiences as a cop had taught me time and time again the value of listening to my instincts. So just what was I in for?

I perched on the edge of my bed and tugged on a boot. Relax, I thought. Put a leash on that imagination of yours. My unease stemmed from a text sent three days earlier. Deputy Chief Tom Franz and the lieutenant over the motor squad, Larry Ewing, wanted to see me. "Don't worry," the deputy chief had said in a follow-up text. "We just want to talk."

Just talk? Like I'd walk into the deputy chief's office and he'd smile and say, "Hi, Eric, how are the wife and kids? You have four little ones, right? Gosh, they grow fast, don't they? Okay, have a safe shift and catch some bad guys. Buh-bye."
I studied my uniform in the bedroom mirror: crisp blue shirt, tan pants with a blue pinstripe down the leg, black boots that gleamed like moonlight on still black water. The uniform had to always be in order. You'd get yourself a dollar fine if you appeared the least bit messy.

I cocked my head to the side and squinted. That person in the uniform, me, thirty-three-year-old Officer Eric Moutsos, looked wrong. I stood too rigid, lips too tight, fists clenched. I slung my black leather utility belt around my hips. The belt felt heavier than usual. Strange. I didn't add anything to it.

Lost in thought, I wandered to the kitchen. Had anyone else been asked recently to chat with the deputy chief and lieutenant? As I concocted a smoothie for lunch, my four kids jabbered, swirled, and scampered around me, disappearing and reappearing as if by magic. Ava, my eldest at age nine, said something about her reading. Seven-year-old Devery asked a question. I muttered an answer.

Whir-whir-whir went the blender. Whir-whir-whir went my mind. When I spoke, my words seemed to drift out of somebody else's mouth. I couldn't quite focus on what my kids said. Why did I feel out of breath?

The reasonable side of me believed the meeting would be about giving me a choice. Perhaps there would be discipline involved, depending on which way I went, or how I came across, but not likely. I envisioned the most probable outcome distilled to: Follow your orders or leave the motorcycle squad and go back to patrol. Administration's message would be clear: Your conscience is irrelevant; orders trump personal beliefs. Slap on the wrist. Bad Eric.

I'd worked so hard to finally be a part of the motorcycle squad. I loved that BMW. Such a beautiful machine, to be sure, but it was more than that. The motorcycle represented challenge and accomplishment. Motor squad stood a step below SWAT as the elite of our police department in my mind.

Few spots opened up and, when they did, a whole lot of officers applied. Only a few ever passed the rigorous requirements. At least two or three officers per class would break bones during the training school and never make it out in one piece.

I marveled at the times I'd ridden on the freeway, in a chain of nearly thirty officers, an exhilarating pride swelling my chest near to bursting. I adored riding on a pleasant night, often thinking, "They are actually paying me to ride a motorcycle." I discovered fulfillment in nabbing a drunk driver, getting him or her off the road, feeling like I'd made a difference, maybe saved a life.

Dear Father in Heaven, what should I do? That had been my fervent prayer the last few days. Should I do the assignment despite my misgivings or risk getting booted back to patrol? Motor squad or my morals? What meant more to me? What would the bigger, long-term consequences be? If I refused, would I hurt my chances for future promotions? The repercussions of my decisions not only affected me, but affected my family, too.

My wife, Stacey, stood between me and the front door. She was as beautiful at thirty as she was on the day we wed. She hugged me and whispered, "It's going to be okay." We held each other and we said a prayer for peace and comfort. By the front door, I kissed my wife and hugged my kids. "Be safe, Daddy," Devery said.

As I sat on my motorcycle and strapped my helmet on, I noticed my family watching from the front porch. They granted me courage and so much more. I managed a smile. Then, that beautiful sound: my motorcycle engine ripped the warm afternoon air. I noticed three-year-old Chris staring at my bike. I flashed my lights and then I was cruising.

The distance to work was twenty-three miles but I didn't mind, especially not on a picturesque day like today. No jacket needed. The perfect way to start a shift. *This is the last time you'll be on a motorcycle.* The intruding thought melted my smile. I squeezed my handlebars and thought, *No, I've earned this. I've worked hard. I've sacrificed. I've risked my life. I—*

Memories sped over my mind the way my bike sped over the highway. They were fond recollections, but now, somehow, they were corroded, tainted by something I couldn't name, something dark, something capable of turning fondness into a taunt. I saw myself new in the Police Academy. The rewarding demands of Field Training. My first arrest. My time on the Bicycle Squad. The day I—

"Eric!" I shouted silently at myself. *"Stop it. Quit worrying. You're going to either do the assignment or go back to patrol; it's not the end of the world."* Still, the dark thoughts nipped at the edges of my consciousness like a chilly fall breeze.

I approached the new Salt Lake City Public Safety Building, a sprawling, curving structure of mostly glass that Salt Lake City PD shared with the Fire Department. I forcibly swallowed the lump in my throat. Was this what the criminals I'd arrested felt as they shuffled into the courtroom for sentencing?

I coasted down the ramp to police underground parking. My engine reverberated, louder and prouder, until I found my stall and killed the engine. I swung off my seat and immediately noticed two other motor cops staring at me. They began to whisper. I frowned, shook my head and told myself to ignore them; get to the meeting. My stupid imagination wanted me to believe they were talking about me. That's all.

I rode the elevator to the 4th floor and when I got off, I saw Sergeant Tim Porter, currently over Internal Affairs, and someone I considered a friend, striding my way, heading for the elevator. "How ya doing sergeant?" I said. He said nothing as he walked by. His expression, however, said a lot. It said, "I know something you don't and I can't bring myself to tell you what." The inside of my mouth turned to cotton; my stomach lurched and twisted. I turned down the next hall and had a straight shot view of my destination.

The door hung open. The Deputy Chief occupied a corner office, the largest on the floor, with an incredible view of downtown Salt Lake City. Deputy Chief Franz wasn't at his desk. Instead, he and Lieutenant Ewing sat side-by-side on cushy chairs, facing the door. They were laughing. "Oh," I thought, and straightened. "This is good. If I was in deep trouble, why would they be laughing?" "Moutsos," the deputy chief said, "Come in. Close the door. Have a seat." He gestured to a chair that faced them.

I closed the door, but hesitated before sitting. I started to raise my right hand, but realized neither of them had moved from their chairs to greet me, which felt odd. Shouldn't we begin a meeting by shaking hands? I wiped my palm on my pants and sat.

The deputy chief straightened, somehow looming while still sitting. He was in his late forties and very physically fit, the kind of guy who liked to check out his muscular arms in mirrors as he passed. Lieutenant Ewing was in his sixties, a balding, gray scarecrow. He should have retired fifteen years ago.

There was no more laughter; no more smiles. Sudden, stifling silence surrounded us. My stomach reached down and strangled my intestines. My pulse skyrocketed. The deputy chief looked me in the eye and said, "What do you want to do about people making fun of you for your religion?"

My mind screeched to a halt. I blinked and tried to reorient myself. This wasn't the topic that I'd anticipated. This was not about the annual Utah Gay Pride Parade. This was about the recent verbal complaint I'd made to my supervisor.

What did I want to do? The question hovered between my ears. I didn't want to punish those who'd harassed me. They probably mocked my religion out of ignorance more than spite. Didn't they? I just wanted us all to be friends, or at least be respectful of one another. Nobody had to agree with my beliefs. You could get along with someone without agreeing with everything they believed. I didn't mind the occasional joke. But the teasing had become tedious, too much, too aggressive. Take it down a notch, that's all. We were on the same team.

Finally, I shook my head and cleared my throat. "Nothing," I said. "I don't want to do anything about it. I just want them to stop and move on. Just realize there's a line where enough is enough."

"Okay," the chief said quickly, chipperly, and patted his thighs twice in rapid succession. His obvious relief left me bewildered. I wondered if I'd saved him some serious paperwork, or maybe he'd been worried about a harassment lawsuit. "Second item of business," the deputy chief said. He leaned forward, expression souring. "I'm afraid you're being placed on administrative leave. For discrimination."

I opened my mouth, but nothing came out. I was about to say, "No, sir, I just want you to talk to them, not seriously discipline them," but then his words sank in. No, not them. Me. On administrative leave? I felt like I was in a parallel dimension. This looked like our world, but everything proceeded upside down and inside out. I tried to start to explain myself. I couldn't articulate anything. I was paralyzed.

This meeting was about the parade after all. But why administrative leave? For asking to trade assignments with someone? I suspected a stern-faced lecture with a lot of finger shaking in my direction. Maybe a written reprimand. Not this. Never this. Had I fooled myself so completely? Had I been so naive? "It's above our heads," the deputy chief said. He shook his head and clicked his tongue. "I wish the lieutenant and I could tell you how we really feel about this."

I glanced at the lieutenant, who was swatting at a fly that kept landing on his head. I wanted to yell at him. This was my job. My life. The least he could do was pay attention. The world around me slowed; my thoughts accelerated, so fast they tripped over each other and accomplished nothing.

The deputy chief held up a paper and began to read. I couldn't follow everything he said, but I understood the gist of it: I couldn't act or perform any type of police duty. The deputy chief said, "As of right now, you are not a police officer. Do you understand?"

I wanted to demand something, but I only felt my head bob. They were slapping me with the severest discipline possible, one step short of being outright fired. For what? For following the dictates of my conscience? They were punishing me for trying to live my faith.

I seemed to skip forward in time. My immediate supervisor, Sergeant Jackman, was suddenly in the office. The forty-five-year old veteran of the force looked worn and creased, brown eyes red and watery. What they were doing to me wounded him. I felt a little less alone, and, despite my turmoil, my hand twitched with a desire to give his shoulder a comforting squeeze.

I found myself removing my gun and handing it to Deputy Chief Franz. Why was I giving him my gun? Oh, right. He asked for it. From the corner of my eye, I noticed the lieutenant held his right hand on his sidearm, as if he didn't know me, as if I was a criminal being arrested and I might pull a weapon and attack.

I looked down to remove the badge pinned to my shirt directly over my heart. Tears splashed off the metal shield. More tears darkened my shirt. I was crying. When had I started to cry? I squeezed my eyes shut, then blinked rapidly to clear my vision. I swayed to my feet, removed my duty belt, and surrendered that, too.

Then I was outside of the office with my sergeant. He swallowed hard, nodded, then escorted me along a familiar route, a path I'd taken so many times, to the motorcycle shed. I had a bizarre, gut-gnawing sensation, like I was heading to a viewing to say goodbye to a dead loved one.

A mini intake room lurked beside the motor office. It was used to temporarily secure a prisoner. I pictured my sergeant shoving me inside and locking the door. A primal part of my mind wanted me to bolt, just run and run and run. But no, my sergeant led me inside the office, a spartan room with only two long desks, a few computers, a copier, and filing cabinets for paperwork.

To my immediate discomfort, six motor cops were inside— or were there seven? Why was I having trouble counting them? Maybe because I couldn't make eye contact, like our gazes were the repelling ends of magnets. Or was it because my vision blurred with tears? Why did they have to be here right now?

I managed a glance at Officer Giles' face and I knew that they knew. Did everyone know? Word of who was placed on administrative leave traveled almost as fast as a dispatched call on the radio for shots fired or an officer down. Who was on leave this week? Gossip, gossip, gossip. Officer Moutsos on administrative leave. Shame. What did he do? Well, I'll tell you what I heard.

I removed my jacket, gloves, and glasses from my locker. Sergeant Jackman led me to my police car and I retrieved my phone charger. "Is that it, Eric?" my sergeant said, almost a whisper. I nodded. He led me to his car. I stared at the badge painted on the side of the door and the words: Salt Lake City Police.

My cell phone buzzed. I flinched then fumbled for the phone in my pocket. My wife. I clenched my teeth. I didn't want her to know; I wanted to spare her the pain. I drew a long, deliberate breath and tried to sound calm. "I'm on my way home." "What do you mean?" "You know what I mean. I…I can't talk now."

My sergeant and I got into his car. After a moment of staring straight ahead, he glanced at me. "You'll get through this." I blinked at his forced smile. He tried again. "You'll be back in no time." "You don't understand," I said. "It's over." His features hardened. I knew that hard gleam in his eyes: hatred for injustice and a determination to avenge. "Please," I said, "don't try to fight for me. You only have a year until retirement. If you try to do anything, they'll come after you, too."

And they would. I understood something with sudden clarity. It was as if I'd been standing an inch from a painting and suddenly stepped back, seeing it for the first time, seeing the whole picture. What I'd done, I'd done tactfully and quietly, and it should have gone hardly noticed.
Not a big deal. Officers traded shifts all the time. But upper administration must've been waiting for this kind of opportunity. How could I have been so blind, so naive to the pressure of outside politics?

Someone high up in administration wanted me gone. I'd voiced my opinion regarding certain police practices one time too many. It seemed one couldn't disagree with the department without the department heads taking it as a personal attack. The rumors I'd heard about me, that I'd simply shrugged off as small gossip spread by small people that no one would actually believe, because the truth was so obviously the opposite, suddenly slammed together, forming not isolated, unrelated parts, but a whole and ugly monster.

A recent event blazed in my mind like a flare at night. I was pulling up into my motorcycle stall in the underground parking lot of the police station and stopped, but the heavy bike started to spill to the right. I couldn't hold the motorcycle and it fell, causing a domino effect into three bikes. It was embarrassing, for sure. However, I'd received a letter in my file for a traffic accident in the parking lot. From what I learned later, it was the first time in the department's history that such a letter had been filed for a tip over, despite hundreds of cops having done the same type of thing on their motorcycles. That should've set off alarms that something was going on.

We exited the underground parking and sunshine pounded my achy eyes. I laid my head back against the passenger seat and stared at the inner roof of the car, realizing that on some deeper level, I had known this would happen. My gut had tried to warn me. I should've expected that the sergeant overseeing the Utah Pride Parade would turn this into a witch hunt that upper management would salivate over. It was his personality. The things he'd said, the vibe he sent out...Don't disrespect my authority. Rock my boat and I'll drown your sorry butt. I know who you are and I don't like you.

I considered a letter I'd recently written to Human Resources. If the chief or mayor heard about an employee challenging the fairness of their hiring and promoting practices, they probably wouldn't like it. We merged onto the interstate and I shook my head at the scenery speeding past. All this because I offered to do security for the parade, but didn't want to participate in the actual parade itself.

I grimaced, thinking, *is this the country I live in now? Where's my freedom of speech? Of religion? Of conscience?* Eventually, we pulled up to my house. Sergeant Jackman asked for several items, including my additional work guns and extra badge. He followed me inside.

My wife and all four of our kids were in the kitchen. When my gaze met Stacey's, she convulsed with a sob and her eyes, those beautiful eyes, gushed tears. I wished I could've spared her this. I went upstairs to get all of the equipment. My throat was burning and I started crying again in my room.

My wife stood in the kitchen confused, while Sergeant Jackman repeated, "I'm so sorry for this," over and over.

Tears spilled down his cheeks, too. My poor kids didn't know what to think as they watched me hand my extra badge over to him. All the adults crying. Their mighty dad reduced to this. A thought that would prove horribly prophetic swept through my mind: *This is just the beginning. Brace yourself, Eric. It ain't over. Not by a long shot. It's going to be a fight. A long, hard fight.*

CHAPTER 2

"You gotta keep your head up when you fight; pick your punches."
—EVANDER HOLYFIELD

Peace of Conscience

The fist filled my vision. I ducked, down and to the left. Blood and sweat stung my right eye. I popped up, jabbed with a right hand. My punch glanced off Michael's beefy forearm. His head seemed so far away, maybe because he was about five inches taller than me. He also outweighed me by a lot. He lived close by. We weren't good friends, but we knew each other's names; we smiled and waved when we saw the other in passing.

Michael faked a right, threw a left. He missed. My left punch pounded his ribs. Michael grunted. I grunted and shook my throbbing hand. Hitting this big Polynesian kid was like driving a fist into a tree. But, hey, I was nineteen and . . . stupid. Michael threw a left, but pulled the punch. I overcommitted. His right hook slammed into my jaw. My head snapped back. I wobbled. A punch smashed into the right side of my gut. I staggered. My abs clenched spasmodically and I doubled over. Each breath seemed to be sucked through a narrow tube.

Michael charged. Clumsily, I sidestepped out of reach. Hunched over, I held up a finger. Michael paused, uncertain what to do. Our rules weren't very clear. One of Michael's cousins said, "Hey, Haole, you need to take a break for a diaper change, eh, bra?" Laughter and jeers erupted from the crowd. I glanced at my brother, who held a camera, filming our mutual combat. I grinned savagely, wiped my eyes, and straightened.

This wasn't the first neighborhood fight. We'd been setting these up for months. Five dollars for admission. It was good pocket change for the fighters, sure, but we didn't do it for the money so much as the rush. "Times up, Moutsos," Michael said. "Lights out." He rushed in, fists raised.My uppercut crashed into his jaw. Thwak! I didn't know if the crunching was his jaw or the bones of my hand or both. I sensed the crowd freeze.

Michael staggered back. He cupped his jaw, eyes squeezed shut. He shook his head and muttered, "I think we're done." I sagged with relief. I was running on fumes. I collected my earnings and a number of high-fives and fist-bumps. As I thumbed through my hard-earned cash, my brother and I headed to my old Ford Bronco. Grimacing, grunting, I pulled myself up to the driver's seat. "Is it as much as you thought?" my brother said.

I shrugged and shoved the wad of bills into the sweaty pocket of my Levi's.I looked up and noticed my face in the rearview mirror. I was a mess, scratched and bloody, with an impressive black eye forming. I shook my head and started the engine. I slid a silver hoop earring into my left earlobe, then one in the right.Hitting the gas, we jerked forward and swerved up the street.

———————

I awoke Sunday morning in pain, but not just from the black eye, swollen, bloody gums, aching jaw, aching muscles, aching knuckles...but in pain because of   something deep inside me. I felt a nagging, aching depression that made me fidgety. I had fought for the money, but I fought for something more: to mask the dark feelings in my gut. Was this typical teenage angst or something more?I hadn't slept well.

My family was at church. I slouched on the couch, television on, but I wasn't really watching. I stood and went to the fridge. I stared at the food, then closed the fridge and wandered back to the couch. The doorbell rang. I shuffled to the front door, muttering, "I'm coming. I'm coming."Ding-dong. I yanked open the door. Michael filled my porch.

I hopped back a step. Was he mad about the outcome of the fight? Did he think the way we split the money was unfair? Did he...I squinted at Michael's clothes. He wore a white shirt and tie with slacks. He grinned at me. "Uh," I said, "hey, Mike. Why are you here?" I gripped the edge of the door, ready to slam it shut if he lunged at me. His grin widened, wrinkling the gruesome bruise on his chin. He said, "It's cool, man. Relax."

I nodded, but wasn't entirely convinced this was safe. I was, after all, home alone. Michael said, "It's my mom, bro. That's why I'm here. She saw my face and about beat me down for getting in a fight with you. I told her it wasn't anything personal, just for money. That didn't help." He laughed. I stared at him, unsure whether to speak or slam the door and return to my moping around the empty house.

Michael said, "My mom told me I'm letting down my ancestors and stuff.Then my auntie, she slapped me. She said I should be telling you about God and stuff." He held up a book. "Here, bro, this is for you." "Okay," I said, and accepted the book. "Uh, thanks." Michael beamed. He rose up on his toes, then nodded and turned to leave.I shook my head and closed the door. Just as I locked the door, I heard Michael yelling back at me, "See you around, brother!"

"Sure thing," I said. "See you around." I grunted at the strangeness of this unexpected interaction. I thumbed through the book he'd given me, a book of scripture apparently. I went to my room and tossed the book on top of my dresser. Then I ate a bowl of cereal. I returned to my room. Lying on my bed, I stared at the book on top of my dresser and nibbled my fingernails. For the first time in my life, I had a serious internal dialogue, asking myself, "Where am I going? I'm nineteen. What should I do with my life?"

Wandering aimlessly around my room, I glimpsed myself in the mirror on the back of my door. I stared at my eyes and snarled. I yanked my earrings out and dropped them on top of the dresser. Gripping its edges, I closed my eyes and growled at the despair overwhelming me, the self-loathing suffocating me. I opened my eyes and there was Michael's book. There were the scriptures. I snatched the book, opened it to a random page, and focused on a paragraph. It talked about peace of conscience.

The idea leapt out at me. Aloud, I said, "Peace of conscience." Yes, that's what I wanted, what I needed. My youth seemed suddenly so frivolous, so empty. I felt like I'd been traveling across a wasteland, nothing worthwhile around me, no destination in mind, just wandering aimlessly, accomplishing nothing. It was time to grow up.

I lay in bed with the scriptures, reading with real intent for the first time in my life. I read for hours. I read the next day and the next. The words seeped into my skin, mixed with my blood, and became a part of me. I could not get enough. I was starving and had never realized it until now. What I read changed me. It wasn't an overnight transformation, but I felt like I had a direction, a blueprint for reform.

I'd forever be grateful to a two hundred-pound Polynesian named Michael for giving me a black eye, then giving me a gift that probably saved my life.

CHAPTER 3

*"If you can't figure out your purpose, figure out your passion.
For your passion will lead you right into your purpose."*

—T.D. JAKES

Who Do You Work For?

In 2004, at the age of twenty-three, I strode into the
Salt Lake City Public Safety Building for the first time.
My grin was nearly perpetual. Would this be like the
TV show Cops?

"Where do we go first?" I asked, bouncing on my toes.
Bryce glanced at me from over his shoulder, chuckled,
and said, "Line-up meeting with the Gang Unit." Line-
up meeting, I thought, and envisioned a row of thugs
behind two-way glass, a witness about to identify the
guilty. Instead, we entered something between a class-
room and an office supply closet. Papers, files, note-
books, markers, staplers, wire baskets, so on and so
forth, cluttered desks and tabletops. Confusion
knocked my grin down a notch.

Eight or nine men crowded the walls and tables. The cops in plain clothes, their badges displayed on their belts or hanging from chains around their necks, out-numbered those in uniform. Rival conversations hummed in the air, peppered with sporadic laughter. I hadn't heard that much cussing in years. They dis-cussed the photos of gang members taped to the walls. Intimidating faces, some covered with so many tattoos they appeared more ink than flesh. I just smiled, soak-ing it all in.

Bryce slapped my shoulder. "You ready to go?" I shrugged, trying to act cool, but my stupid grin likely ruined the façade. "Ahh-ya," I said. "Ready when you are." Bryce tossed me a bullet-proof vest. Wow. I thought the cameras were about to roll, like I was in an action film. Bryce and I exited the room and I imag-ined us walking in slow motion, tough guy music in the background. Bryce led me to his car and we met up with his partner, Shawn Wheeler. They sat up front, me in the back. It wasn't long before we had our first call crackle over the radio: Man with a knife at a TRAX light rail station.

It seemed like mere seconds and we were parked near the raised platform where passengers embarked or dis-embarked from the trains. Cars passed on either side, adding an element of danger to the situation. "Stay in the car," Bryce said. I nodded, thinking, Yeah, just like

the movies. No. Better. This was real. I could see everything from where I sat.

Bryce and Shawn approached someone matching the
description dispatch had given: white male in his twenties, black hat and backpack. They chatted with the
guy, then they were searching him, patting him down.
They could've found a bazooka and I wouldn't have
been more excited.

I poked my head between their seats. "What happened?" Bryce snorted and shook his head. "Seems the
guy had a rather large pocket knife sticking out from
under his shirt. Whoever called 911 freaked out over
nothing illegal." I nodded and kept nodding. Okay, so
this wasn't a shoot-out or anything, but still exciting.

Later, after sundown, we stopped for a bar check at a
downtown pub. Still wearing my bulletproof vest, I followed Bryce and Shawn inside. I crossed the threshold
and Techno music thumped my ears; stale hops mixed
with food and a dozen other odors hit my nose; laser
lights crisscrossed the space above heads and shattered
crystal twinkled from a couple disco balls.
Every eye considered us. "5.0 in the house," someone
called. "Hide your weed," a man said, and his friends
laughed. "Oh, someone's in trouble," a woman said.
Shawn leaned towards a guy holding a glass mug, said
something beside his ear, and the guy laughed and
spilled some of his drink.

Time moved too fast; the night ended too soon. I didn't want to go home, but there I was, 3:00 a.m., at my front door, bright-eyed and smiling, sneaking inside my dark house, feeling like a teenager after a date that had led to a first kiss. Oh yes, I was in love.

In our bedroom, Stacey was a dark shape beneath the covers. I couldn't stop myself. I leaned across my side of the bed and shook her shoulder. Her eyes hadn't even opened before I was jabbering about everything that happened. Stacey clicked on her bedside lamp.

"I mean, I never thought about being a cop before, but, babe, I...uh..." The flat, annoyed expression on her face finally registered. I closed my mouth, shrugged, and gave her a sheepish look. "Sorry," I said. "I guess this could've waited until morning." Stacey sighed, touched my arm, and her face softened. "You would make a great cop," she said. That simple statement carried all the approval I needed. I'd do it. I was going into law enforcement. Funny how life takes you places you never expected to go.

———

Hiring on with a police department in Utah proved a lot harder than I anticipated. The competition was fierce with hundreds of applicants for every opening. In 2006, the overall vibe towards law enforcement was still somewhat positive. Cops were your friend. Cops saved lives. Cops kept the peace. Law enforcement didn't seem all that politically polarized. At least not to me.

Committed to my goal of becoming an officer, I decided to increase my likelihood of being hired by putting myself through the police academy. I didn't have the money, so I paid with a credit card: $2,500 for Cat 1 certification then another $2,500 for Cat 2 certification.

My most memorable moment at the police academy came in the form of a special guest speaker. Chief Randy Jacobson of a local police agency, a veteran with nearly forty years of experience, stood behind the lectern of the stage and addressed our class of nearly 20 recruits. He warned us of what we would face as officers, the kinds of people we'd deal with, and the sacred opportunity of helping others. We would see firsthand the hell people can make of their lives and the toll being in law enforcement would take on our own lives. And then, to conclude his remarks, he asked the audience, "Who do you work for?"

Recruits began raising their hands and Chief Jacobson would point and say, "Yes, you." "We work for the people." Chief Jacobson shook his head. "We work for the community." "Yes, yes," he said, "but not the best answer." "I'll work for you, sir," someone said. "Give me a job." Chief Jacobson smiled, rolled his eyes, and waited for the laughter to subside. His expression firmed and his eyes sharpened. Finally, he said, "I want to make this really clear. You work for God, and I never want you to forget it." The auditorium stilled. There was shock on some faces, confusion on others, but mostly there was a sense of weight. Those heavy words pressed down on us. That sentiment penetrated my soul and left a mark on me like nothing else I learned during the next few months at the academy. You work for God.

"Anything I've ever put my mind to," I said, "I've done it." From my side of the desk, I looked up at Chief Cainam, being sure to make eye contact. The man, lanky and near six and a half feet tall, reminded me more of a retired basketball player than a cop. We were on the eighth floor in a large, corner office overlooking the East side of the Salt Lake valley.

"Anything," I continued. "From junior high student body president, to the All-Star Baseball Team, to number one in singles on high school tennis. I even made it on Evander Holyfield's record label and opened up a country show for Collin Raye. Sir, I will be one of the best officers you have."

Chief Cainam smiled in an amused, fatherly way, but also with something I could only interpret as longing. "Collin Raye?" he said. "Really?" "Yes, sir. I enjoy singing." "Well, Eric, I think you will make us proud." Nailed it, I thought, and grinned. Chief Cainam stood and reached his hand across the desk to shake my hand. Then I was gliding out of the office, floating down to ground level, out the double glass doors of the Salt Lake City Police Department building, and into the beautiful spring day.

I couldn't restrain myself. I half jogged, half danced to my white 1998 Chevy Trailblazer. I caught my reflection in the glass of a building on the other side of the sidewalk. I paused beside the driver-side door. I was a young man in a suit and tie, grinning ear-to-ear. I grabbed the front of my shirt and pretended to rip it open, like Clark Kent becoming Superman.
I slapped the top of my car. I had to call Stacey. I had to share this moment of euphoric triumph. Stacey answered. "I got the job!" "Are you serious, babe?" "It's not official, but I know it. I know it." "Oh, that's great. So awesome." "On my way," I said. "See you soon."

CHAPTER 4

"Our lives are a sum total of the choices we have made."
—WAYNE DYER

I Can Only Imagine

My Field Training Officer, or FTO, Adam James, scowled at the traffic ahead of us. His grip tightened on the steering wheel and he muttered, "Shoulda taken State Street."

I smiled at Officer James, then looked out my passenger-side window and up at the Wells Fargo Center, the tallest building in Salt Lake City. I imagined standing on the top-most ledge of that skyscraper, like a superhero surveying the city he must keep safe. My grin widened. I found myself grinning a lot. If anyone ever saw a cop perpetually grinning, he probably wasn't crazy, just a newbie, like I was, still on probation, not yet jaded, every moment a rush. Just putting on my badge in the morning exhilarated me.

My FTO pointed at something ahead. "That guy's probably a pedophile." I flinched, looked, and followed his line of sight to a man waddling across the street at the intersection ahead: forty-something, built like Buddha, but with a scraggly mop of black hair and a bushy mustache. His too-short jean shorts seemed moments from splitting up his flabby white legs.

"You can't really know just by looking," I said. My FTO grunted. "Man, my pedophile radar is bleeping like crazy. Wait and see, Moutsos. Five years bein' a cop and you'll see someone and just know what crime they committed--or are thinking about committing. Of course, you have to prove everything, and all that. Can't just profile. I mean, you could see a sign in the air above some dude's head, clear as day, that says, 'I beat my wife in a rage this morning,' but you can't just tackle the guy and take him to jail. Proof. Always need proof. Articulate, the more the better. Nothing worse than arresting someone you know is guilty and he gets cut loose by the DA because there's not enough proof, or you lose in court, or whatever."

I frowned and thought: *No, I'd stop him before he hurt his wife. Somehow.* Naive. Officer James continued. "You can't just go and start surveillance on somebody's house just because he looks suspicious. Always stay within policy and procedures. You have to be able to articulate everything you do. Anyway, Moutsos, you got some questions?"

"Dozens," I said, and considered where to start. There were hundreds of different types of calls I could find myself on and I needed to pass off several before I could be on my own. "How about handling a barricaded subject?"

Officer James turned right onto 100 South. He nodded at my probation handbook on the floor between my feet. "Look it up. We'll discuss it." I snatched my book and searched the glossary. "Found it," I said. "Barricaded Subject. A barricaded subject can be defined as a person or persons in a location that provides a means of spatial separation that assists them in avoiding apprehension from law enforcement. In short, a barricaded subject is in a position that inhibits law enforcement from easily taking them into custody after they have committed a crime."

James nodded and opened his mouth, but a triple-beep emergency came across our radio from Dispatch. A man with a gun, inside his apartment, refused to surrender to Adult Probation and Parole. James cursed. "That's a block or two away," I said.

James nodded and spoke into his mic. "Dispatch, this is car 84, we're a minute or less away and responding." Our car accelerated. James grunted, glanced my way, then straight ahead. "How's that for irony? A freaking barricaded subject."

James yanked our car into an apartment complex parking lot, maybe sixteen units. The old, yellowing brick structures looked like they should've , everything run down. I spotted no Salt Lake City PD cars. We were the first to arrive. James parked and we shoved out of our car. "There," James said, pointing to a white number 12, the "2" hanging askew.

We'd only taken a few steps when two middle-aged men with Adult Parole and Probation badges turned the corner. The taller AP&P agent held up a hand in greeting. He reminded me of a plump Macaulay Culkin. "What do we got?" James asked. "The usual," the taller agent said. "Mr. Carl Freddy broke probation. We came to pick him up and he's refusing. Says he's armed and won't go back to prison. His front door is one flight up. There's a window on the other side, but I don't see him jumping out. He's not the athletic type. Besides, he probably wouldn't fit through it."

"We're pretty sure he's alone," the shorter agent said as he shook my hand.I hoped he didn't notice how my hands shook with excitement and fear. You shouldn't be afraid as a cop, right? But I was. I'd never been in this type of situation. Barricaded and armed. I gritted my teeth and told myself to focus.Be professional.

"All right," James said. "We got it from here." I followed James through the main entrance, a squeaky gate with more rust than white paint and up the first flight of stairs to the second floor. Muffled yelling leaked through the edges of Freddy's door. James touched my shoulder. I flinched. James nodded to the apartment to the right. "First thing first. Keep everyone safe. See if anyone is home and evacuate them in case this turns ugly. I'll go left."

I nodded and crept to the right. I peeled my fingers off the grip of my Glock 17 and knocked softly. The situation felt surreal, more like a training scenario than reality. I kept glancing at Freddy's door, half expecting him to come out with guns blazing. Part of me wanted to run; part of me wanted to whoop like an excited teenager.

A scruffy, twenty-something Hispanic male peeked out of his apartment."We have a problem next door," I said. The man's eyes jerked towards Freddy's apartment, then back to me. He barked a nervous laugh. "Yeah, man. No kidding." "For your safety, we need you to evacuate. Stay a safe dis-tance away until this is resolved."
He nodded and hurried past me. A woman pushed her two young boys ahead of her and down the stairs. The youngest boy, maybe four, whimpered, his big eyes pulling everything in.James nodded to Freddy's door. The man inside ranted, something about it not being fair.

Officer James and I evacuated the apartments above and below Freddy's, as well. We then took up positions on either side of his door, James to the right, me left. James gripped his holstered gun and knocked with his free hand. "Mr. Freddy. Mr. Freddy, this is Officer James with the Salt Lake City Police Department. We'd like you to come out and talk to us." Freddy yelled, his voice much closer. "I got a shot-gun. I got one. Okay. I'm not going to prison!"

"Mr. Freddy, please, we--" "I'll end it," Freddy screamed. "I'll end it all! I will!" I'd never heard a voice strangled by so much raw emotion. Could we even reason with someone who owned a voice like that? "Mr. Freddy, please calm down. Let's talk about--" Something crashed inside the apartment followed by a wild scream. James keyed his mic. He stepped back. "Dispatch, this is Officer James."A female voice said, "Go ahead, James." "We're at the Freddy address. He's irate, threatening to kill himself. I want you to try to get him on the phone, find a number for him, see if you can calm him down that way."

"Copy, Officer James. We have his contact info and will call." "Great," James said. "If you get through, transfer the call to my cell." I cocked my head. Sirens. Getting closer. Our backup. James pointed to the apartment to the left of Freddy's. "Go inside. See if you can hear through the wall, figure out where he is in his apartment."I nodded.

James' cell phone buzzed and he picked up. "Hello, is this Carl Freddy?" I crept inside the Hispanic male's apartment, following the wall they shared, past the living room with a single sofa and into the kitchen and dining area.For a moment, all I heard was my own breathing, then a man's voice, muffled. Freddy. I thought, *If he knew I was here, he could blast right through that thin wall with his shotgun.* I shoved the thought aside and focused. I turned my radio down and slowed my breathing.

"I did it," Freddy said, nearly shouting. "I did it. I couldn't help it. You know? I should've gotten rid of my computer, just threw it away." His voice trembled. "Yeah, that's why AP&P wanted me. They know what's on my computer. They know about the child porn. What? No!" I realized Freddy was talking to someone on his phone. Silence for a few seconds, then a scream. I flinched again.

"It's over! It's over! I can either go back to prison or kill myself. Those are my options. You don't have any other options. I know you don't. No, I won't listen. You...What? Who wants to talk to me?" Freddy sobbed. I winced. "Hey," someone whispered. "Moutsos." James stood in the doorway, waving me over. As I hurried to him, in a low voice, he said, "I gave the phone to the negotiators. SWAT is below."

A deep, distant thumping reached my ears. I cocked my head. "Is that a helicopter?" James scowled, listened, waved my question away, and said, "Come on." I followed my trainer down the stairs. SWAT members in black and armed like a military assault force jogged past us. A helicopter thumped and whirred overhead. It wasn't law enforcement. It was KSL's Chopper 5. Local news.

James led me to Sergeant Grow, who was leaning in and conversing with Lieutenant Vanscoy. Sergeant Grow noticed us, nodded, and raised his voice to be heard over the helicopter. "You two, on perimeter, there and there." The lieutenant said, "Somebody get that chopper away. I can't hear my own radio."

I headed for the north side of the apartment complex. I had a good view of the rear of the apartments and found the back window AP&P had mentioned.Time crawled. I kept thinking that something should be happening. The negotiators must be having a lovely conversation with--Boof!

I flinched, dropped my center of gravity, and had my gun part way out of the holster. Shotgun. He had a shotgun, right? The noise had to be a shotgun. Was someone shot? The suspect? An officer? I stepped towards the apartment, then halted. There was nothing I could do. Just wait. My nerves seemed to spark inside my body; my muscles felt stretched and desperate for release. Action. Any action. I wanted to help, but held my position. Nothing on the radio.

Three SWAT members jogged around the corner. They halted below Freddy's rear window and one raised a round mirror on an extendable pole. He peeked inside from a safer position, below and to the side. My radio crackled. A male voice said, "Suspect is down. Appears to be a self-inflicted wound to the head. Secure the scene and get medical inside."

The suspect was down, not an officer. I closed my eyes and exhaled a long breath. Not the best outcome, but better than a dead comrade. An ambulance that had been waiting on the street pulled forward and disappeared around the front of the apartment complex. No, not the best outcome.

The man made his choice, I thought. He made a lot of wrong choices.Somewhere, somehow, he got into child porn. How does someone even do that? I wondered if I should be glad this pedophile was gone from the world, but I lacked the emotional energy to rejoice. I held only a hollow nausea in my gut with an underlying sense of relief.

A few minutes later, Mr. Freddy was pronounced dead. Personnel trickled off the scene. "Officer Moutsos," Officer James said through my radio."Go ahead." "You're done with perimeter. Meet me at the front of the apartment.""Copy."
I shuffled around to the front of the building and ducked under the yellow and black tape that marked the area as a crime scene.

James nodded in greeting, then jerked a thumb in the direction of Freddy's open front door. "It'll be a good experience to check out the crime scene. You good with that?" I nodded. At the threshold, I hesitated. Suddenly conflicted, I was apprehensive yet curious. A dead body waited in there. *Just go*, I told myself. *Don't be a wuss.*

I entered the sparsely furnished apartment and heard music drifting out of a room from the hall ahead. I frowned, recognizing the song. It belonged to a Christian band called MercyMe. The song was "I Can Only Imagine." I passed the kitchen and into the hall. Bathroom on one side, bedroom on the other. I smelled Freddy first: the sharp tang of urine mixed with the coppery reek of blood and a hint of burnt hair.

Grimacing, I stepped inside the bedroom and arrived in what seemed another world. The body lay slumped on its belly beside the bed's footboard. As I blinked at what remained of the head, which wasn't much, MercyMe sang:

> What will my heart feel
> Will I dance for you Jesus
> Or in awe of You be still
> Will I stand in your presence
> Or to my knees will I fall
> Will I sing hallelujah
> Will I be able to speak at all
> I can only imagine

The song repeated, set on a loop by the dead man, playing on a speaker hooked to his phone, which lay beside it on the nightstand. Go to prison or die. He had believed that those were his only options. And the truth is, they were.

But I realized he was already a prisoner, having bound himself with all of his choices, spread across all of his years. Even when he'd been free on the outside, he couldn't be free on the inside. I'd been taught that laws, on this earth and in the universe, weren't so much about restricting us, but keeping us free of the greater restrictions that come from the consequences of those broken laws. The laws Freddy broke led him down a path that turned him into the most reprehensible of addicts, the one who craved the flesh of children. Revolting and tragic.

My shoulders sagged. I turned and trudged away, relieved to abandon the pedophilic corpse. The memories of my first dead body, however, were not so easily left behind. What was seen could never be unseen.

CHAPTER 5

"Our prayers may be awkward. Our attempts may be feeble. But since the power of prayer is in the one who hears it and not in the one who says it, our prayers do make a difference."

—MAX LUCADO

Pray to Find a Bad Guy

Snow crunched beneath my boots. The wind bit the exposed skin of my face and yanked aside the steamy plumes of my exhaled breath. I halted and squinted at what the medical examiners heaved onto the shore of the Jordan River. It was January 2008.

Roughly two weeks ago, a drunken man had called Salt Lake City Police, muttering nearly incoherently about a body in the Jordan River, something about pushing her in and wanting police to find her and tell her husband. Officers searched later that night, but found nothing.

Not long after that, two boys playing near the Utah State Fair park after school spotted what they thought was a mannequin bobbing along the river.Naturally, the boys threw rocks at it. One of the boys started to believe it might be a real body. He later stopped a policeman who was driving through his neighborhood.

Now we were here. I frowned at the bluish corpse and wondered how the boys had ever believed that was anything but a real body. My trainer, Officer Zabian, appeared beside me. He nodded at the deceased."Good thing that water is near slush or there'd be little more than gelatin on a skeleton. Preserved like that, I bet we ID her." Disgust twisted my lips nearly to a snarl. I wanted to find whoever had done this to that poor woman.

A few days later at our start-of-shift lineup meeting, our sergeant announced that the woman found in the Jordan River was forty-year-old Barbara J Roland, a transient who sometimes stayed at homeless shelters. Autopsy showed the cause of death as blunt force trauma to the head. Her husband, Bradford Roland, was a person of interest, but was M.I.A.

After the meeting, while I waited for my training officer, I crossed paths with one of the veteran motorcycle officers, affectionately nicknamed Dudley.He had moved from Oklahoma with an accent to prove it. He was one of the shortest officers in the department but, man, how he could ride a motorcycle. Incredible on and off the road. We got along fantastic, both of us playing guitar and singing country music.

We chatted for a couple minutes, then I asked, "You hear anything about that homeless woman found in the river, or her husband?" Dudley opened his mouth as if to speak, but then looked at the ground between us. I waited. And waited. I glanced both directions, then opened my mouth to ask if everything was okay, but he finally looked up and spoke. "Moutsos, you ever prayed to find a bad guy?"

I blinked, unsure what to say. I thought maybe he was kidding, but his expression was earnest, his gaze unwavering. I cleared my throat. "Uh, what do you mean?" "I mean exactly what I said. You ever prayed to find a bad guy? It works.Look, I know you believe in God. I do, too. I swear He wants to help us."Dudley shrugged and lowered his voice to barely more than a whisper. "If we let Him. You pray, right?" I nodded.

Dudley said, "Before every shift, I ask God to lead me to people who need my help. I plead with the good Lord above to help me find the bad guys. Make the world safer for all His children." We stood together in silence for a moment and then Dudley glanced past me. "I'll see ya around, Moutsos. Be safe." "Thanks," I said. "You, too."

Dudley left, but his words remained with me. Officer Zabian slapped my shoulder. "You ready, greenie?" I grinned. "Of course."

That night, driving home, my thoughts slipped back to what Dudley had said about praying to find the bad guys. I thought again of Chief Jacobsen telling us at the academy that we work for God, not for him or the department or even the community. Never forget that.

A sliver of guilt poked at my insides. Dudley was right. I should've been praying that same type of prayer since the day I started. Sure, I often asked my Heavenly Father for help with my job, but I'd never been so specific, so focused.

After arriving at home, kissing Stacey, and changing into my sweatpants, I sneaked to the bedroom where my kids slept. Assigned to the swing shift, my two girls were usually asleep by the time I arrived. I peeked inside and studied their peaceful faces; I listened to their soft, consistent breathing. Something within my chest swelled and warmed. In a way, when I worked to keep Salt Lake City safe, I was really trying to keep these sleeping angels safe.

I returned to my bedroom where Stacey sat up in bed, reading. "I had this conversation with Dudley today." "Dudley?" she said with a quizzical grin, and lowered her magazine. "Like Dudley Do-Right? Perfect name for a cop." I snorted a laugh, shook my head, and told her about our conversation.

"Dudley is wise," Stacey said, smirking, then turning a bit serious. "You should do it. More often than not, God works through people to answer other people's prayers, right? Why wouldn't God help you when what you do is so important?" I grinned. "You're so very wise."

Stacey shrugged nonchalantly. "I am the best thing to ever happen to you.""Can't argue with you there," I said. "Are you ready for bed? I'm exhausted."Stacey set her magazine on the nightstand and said, "Your turn to say prayers."

I paused for a moment, deep in thought. My voiced edged to heaven through the silent room. I ended my prayer with, "Father, please, help me find the person who killed the lady in the river."

———◦◦◦◦———

The next couple of days as part of our lineup meetings, Barbara Roland been located. I kept a prayer in my heart that I, or someone else, would find him.
February 7, 2008, Officer Zabian and I were in our car. As Zabian drove and I peered out the window at the passing cars, I experienced the inexplicable.I could see in my mind the sudden picture of a cafeteria at a homeless shelter. I knew the place and I knew Bradford Roland was there. I was as certain of that as of the fact that I was sitting on a seat in a moving car.

"Go to the homeless shelter on Rio Grande," I said. Zabian glanced sideways at me, his forehead furrowed. "Now? Why?" Despite my trainer's expression and the note of incredulity in his voice, I didn't back down. I couldn't doubt the quiet certitude of that whisper in the back of my head. "We need to go there. Now. They're serving dinner. We need to get there before they finish."

Zabian stared ahead for a moment, then shrugged. "Okay," he said, then muttered, "Nothing better to do." But he didn't speed up. My fingers drummed against my knees. I wanted to flip on the lights and sirens and shout, "Go, go, go!"

My mood finally infected Zabian. He sped up a bit, then a bit more. We rushed along 200 South, then turned down Rio Grande Street and parked in front of the shelter. My heart drummed at the base of my throat. Was I crazy? Was this a mistake? No. I knew he was there. Bradford Roland was there. Inside. Right now.

I released my seatbelt and sprang from the warm car into the frigid winter. Zabian locked gazes with me and cocked an eyebrow as if to say: Go ahead. This was your bizarre idea. I swallowed, nodded, and strode towards the entrance. Clumps of homeless in winter gear and multiple layers of clothing stood or sat along the sidewalk. Their suspicious eyes seemed to drill holes in the sides of my head.
If I was wrong, I'd look like a fool. *No. He's in there.*

People of different races, sexes, and degrees of hygiene stepped aside as we entered the shelter and walked down the hall, some muttering, some glaring. At one time or another, a high percentage of these people had been arrested or cited by Salt Lake City PD, by officers like us.

We entered the clinking and clanking, rustling and bustling of the cafeteria. The odors of boiling pasta and simmering sauce with an underlying stench of body odor clogged my nostrils. I scanned the rows of people sitting on benches at the tables, eating their dinner. Those nearest and facing us froze and then it spread, like ripples in a pond -- that startled look, then a mix of reactions from curious to hostile.

I headed to the nearest table, focused on two scruffy, older men sitting side-by-side, hunched and wheezing with laughter. A few feet away, I hit a potent wall of alcohol fumes and stale sweat. I hesitated, and considered approaching someone else, but now the two were blinking up at me with red-rimmed eyes.

I nodded to the men, rounded the table, and stood across from them. "Do you guys know Bradford Roland?" They blinked at me. They blinked at each other. And then they burst into raucous laughter, one of them slamming his fist down on the tabletop, again and again, rattling cups and plates. I sighed and looked around for someone else I could approach.

A blue latex glove reached around my right shoulder. I flinched. My right hand jerked to my gun and I thought, *He could've grabbed my gun.* I wasn't paying attention to my surroundings. Stupid. The hand grabbed an abandoned tray beside the two men I'd spoken to and I twisted to look up at the man in the gloves. "Have you guys found my wife yet?" the man asked.

A chill ran up my spine and goosebumps pricked my arms. *No*, I thought. *No way.* I said, "You're Bradford Roland." "Yeah," he said. "Put the tray down and put your hands behind your back." "But have you found her?" he said. Officer Zabian, his expression incredulous, almost comical, crept up behind Roland. He glanced at me then back to Roland and shook his head. I raised my handcuffs. Roland offered me his wrists. The cuffs clicked and ratcheted tight. I exhaled a deep breath and wondered if this was a dream.

We called for the homicide detectives to come and interview Roland, then Zabian and I escorted him to our car. Along the way, my trainer kept glancing at me from the other side of Roland, his expression saying, "What the crap just happened, Moutsos? Is this real?" I could only give a little shrug, unsure how to explain this.

We placed Roland in the back of the car, got in ourselves, and started our report. Homicide arrived shortly and we turned Bradford Roland over to them for questioning. He would confess that night to murdering his wife and tossing her body into the Jordan River.

After a sincere prayer of gratitude for God's help and inspiration, I called Dudley. He deserved to know the truth of what happened. "Dudley," I said, "you're never going to believe this." I was wrong. Dudley did believe, and that felt good.

CHAPTER 6

"People call me wild. Not really though, I'm not. I guess I've never been normal, not what you call Establishment. I'm country."

—JOHNNY CASH

Karaoke Cop and Thor

Every couple of weeks, a new officer, like me, was assigned to a different partner. This evening, I felt like I'd been assigned to Thor. I was in awe. I knew I could learn a lot from a guy like this, a veteran, in more ways than one. Not only did he have twelve years of experience with Salt Lake City PD, but he also belonged to the United States Army Rangers, a Black Beret.

Currently, he worked on SWAT and the Gang Unit. Not only mentally tough, by all accounts, but physically. I'd stumbled across this guy at the gym, not just doing pull-ups, but pull-ups with a forty-five-pound plate hanging from a rope around his waist, rep after rep, like it was nothing. If we got in a tight spot, I doubted there was anyone better to have my back.

With my partner at the wheel, we drove around Salt Lake City, patrolling, listening for the next call, car radio scanning. Not long after dark, we picked up a vehicle pursuit in a neighboring city, but heading towards Salt Lake. The suspect was wanted for aggravated assault on a police officer. He drove a blue Dodge Durango. My partner perked up, glanced sideways at me and grinned like a wolf who'd spotted a lame deer. Delicious, fresh meat, within reach. The pursuit was Northbound on I-15, not far from us, so we headed for the freeway.

My excitement deflated a bit when my partner turned onto the exit ramp for 1300 South. It wasn't a big exit and, though possible, I believed it an unlikely choice for the suspect. My partner positioned our car behind a wall and turned off the lights. We leaned towards the car radio. Our eyes scanned the top of the off ramp.The pursuit neared our location. "A blue Dodge Durango," my partner whispered. "Come on, baby. Come to papa."

The pursuit passed the 21st South exit. I swallowed, thinking, *What if he did exit here?* An SUV, lights off, shot down the 1300 South off ramp. I snapped to rigid attention. "Dodge Durango." The vehicle zipped past like a bobsled in the Winter Olympics. Our engine roared. Tires screeched. The acceleration and turn shoved me back against my seat. The Durango jerked right, fleeing east on 1300 South. We followed.

The Durango careened through a four-way stop. At the intersection, we screeched to a slower speed, checked left and right, then leapt forward. We hit speeds on a thirty-five-mph road that I would rather not admit to. I clung with both hands to the passenger-side roof handle and my heels dug into the floor mat, lifting my butt off the seat. Car chases on TV and in movies thrilled me. This did not thrill me. I had zero control.

I glanced at my partner. His left hand held the wheel; his right hand keyed the radio mic on his shoulder. He growled something, but his words didn't register in my mind. I realized he was now talking to me, not the radio."Moutsos, what are you doing?" I said, "Please don't kill us." He barked a laugh. I didn't smile.

The faces of my wife and kids shuffled through my mind. Ahead, the Durango slowly shrunk. Four blocks. Five blocks. We were losing him. The lunatic didn't slow for anything, not stop signs, not red lights. Safety--and sanity--required us to approach intersections with caution or risk a collision, or hit a pedestrian.

The Watch Commander's voice came across the radio. "All officers, terminate the pursuit. There's too much risk to public safety. End the pursuit." We slowed and pulled over. I exhaled and slumped against my seat, limp as a wet rag. "You can pull your underwear out of your crack now," my partner said. I laughed. He laughed.

After a minute to collect our thoughts and allow the adrenaline to fade, we started driving, leisurely. I felt like we'd gone from a monster roller coaster to a merry-go-round for toddlers.

My partner glanced at me and said, "So, the rumor is you were a country singer before becoming a cop." "Yep," I said. "Kinda seems like another life now." "You had something to do with Evander Holyfield?" I nodded. "He has a record label. I performed under the name 'Eric Ryan'."My partner barked a laugh. "No kidding. The Champ has a record label?""He does," I said. "A good guy, Evander." My partner eyed me a moment then said, "Well, let's hear you." I chuckled and shook my head.

He flashed a predatory grin. "You're serious?" I said. "I'm the senior officer here.
I say you sing." "I'm the senior officer here. I say you sing." I grimaced out my window. "Well, I don't have any music on hand." My partner turned the car, heading north.

I thought about the chance I once had at a country music career. Sometimes I missed singing, but I'd decided it wasn't the kind of life I wanted for my young family, so I walked away. I knew, deep in my gut, it had been the right choice. I belonged here. I'd be a good officer.

My partner pulled over to the curb alongside a busy down-town bar. He killed the engine. "What are we doing?" I asked. He grinned and the intense gleam in his eyes made me wary. He pointed at the window of the bar. "We're going to hear you sing." I rolled my eyes. "No," he said. "Really." I opened my mouth, but no words came out. My gaze followed the line of his finger to the window. A single word blazed in neon lighting: Karaoke."No," I said. "Please, no."

My partner leaned towards me and waggled his eyebrows. He got out and walked around the car, watching me with a disconcerting grin. He opened my door and gestured for me to exit. I hesitated. He waited. "Fine," I said, and exited the car, thinking that he had to have some other reason for being here. I knew he was toying with the new guy, that was all. I followed him inside. The lighting was dim. Music and singing; the buzz of conversations. Beer and the aroma of burgers and fries. The average-sized bar was packed. Every seat was taken and many patrons were standing.

As usual, when people noticed us, they stopped talking and stared with a mix of wariness and curiosity. "What are they doing here?" "Hey, it's the cops." "Dude, check it out." I turned back to my partner, but he was gone. I craned my neck, scanning the crowd, and finally spotted him near the small stage near the back of the bar. He leaned in, talking to the DJ. *Oh, no*, I thought. *He really is serious. This isn't a random bar check.*

My partner strode my way, caught my eye, and grinned. He held up a small, black book and a white slip of paper. "This isn't happening," I said. "Oh," my partner said, "it's happening. Who do you like?" "What?" "Who do you like? What artist do you like?" "Uh," I said. "Johnny Cash. I guess."

My partner opened the book. He shoved it into my hands. "Write down a song from the book on the paper. C'mon. C'mon." "Okay, okay," I said and skimmed through the lists of artists and songs. "Folsom Prison Blues" leapt off the page. I wrote it down on the slip of paper. My partner snatched the book and paper, grinned, slapped my shoulder, and hurried back to the DJ, nearly knocking a young woman over in the process.

I watched my partner's back, hoping he'd turn around and say, "Joke's on you. You don't have to sing." Deep down, I knew he really was messing with me and wouldn't force me to sing, but I decided to go ahead and do it. I wasn't going to turn back at that point.

Laughter to my right tugged my attention that way. A group of men and women were conversing excitedly, a guy pointing at my partner, then all of them looking at me, then back at the stage. My heart pumped faster. I closed my eyes, breathed in, then exhaled a long breath. I told myself not to worry. A place packed like this, Karaoke Night, probably a wait of an hour before I had to sing. We'd probably get a call on the radio to respond somewhere before then and I'd be--

"Next up," the DJ said, cooing into his microphone, "Officer Eric with Salt Lake PD." The packed bar hushed, everyone still. Into the silence, two glasses clinked. I grimaced at my audience, then noticed my partner. I scowled and shook my head, but he just waved me over.

I dragged my feet forward, weaving my way between several groups. I mouthed a silent, brief prayer, "Please, God help me not to embarrass myself and the department."From beneath his trim beard, the DJ flashed delighted white teeth. He offered me the mic with a bow and a flourish of his hands. I muttered, "I'm going to get fired for this." "Light it up," the DJ said, and raised his hands in the air.

I planted my feet on the stage and faced a hushed crowd swollen with excitement and ready to burst. Even the bartenders had stopped their furious drink-pouring to watch. I hoped the karaoke machine didn't suck, and you never knew what you'd get with karaoke tracks. A crackle from the speakers. The twang of Johnny Cash's guitar. The volume was good, just about right in the near silence. The first lyrics filled the room. "I hear the train a comin'. It's rollin' round the bend." I realized it was me singing.

"And I ain't seen the sunshine since I don't know when." The crowd leaned forward. They were a shoreline of widening eyes and parting lips. "I'm stuck in Folsom Prison and time keeps draggin' on. But that train keeps a rollin' on down to San Anton." The bar erupted. Whoops and cheers; claps and whistles. I grinned and sang on. "When I was just a baby, my momma told me, 'Son. Always be a good boy. Don't ever play with guns.'"

A man and woman climbed atop a table and started dancing. Others followed their lead. The crowd surged closer, crowding the small stage. I closed my eyes, feeling the twanging guitar, giving the song a bit of my heart and soul. "And I'd let that lonesome whistle, blow my blues away." The song ended. The crowd roared with approval, shrill whistling and applause. I raised my hands and gestured for quiet. After a minute, the crowd stilled enough to hear my voice through the speakers.

Considering how this might somehow make it to my supervisor, I decided to turn all public service announcement, like this was some kind of community-oriented policing performance. I said, "There's gonna be no drinking and driving tonight, right?" The crowd cheered and laughed. I handed the microphone back to the beaming DJ, who clapped me on the back, turned to the crowd, and said, "Wow! How about that. Give Officer Eric a hand."

The crowd thundered approval. I found my partner, who stood at the end of a nearby table holding his stomach with one hand, pounding the top of the table with the other, and roaring with laughter. People approached me, waving their phones, smiling and asking for a picture with the country-singing cop. I shook hands, fist-bumped, and high-fived my way to the exit.My partner appeared at my side, threw an arm across my shoulders, squeezed and laughed. "Ah, man. Eric, bro, you exceeded my expectations. That was great. We made some great bridges with the community." He couldn't stop grinning. Frankly, neither could I.

Not long after leaving the bar, we returned to our substation to eat and relax for a few minutes. As soon as we entered the break room, my partner clapped once, whooped, laughed, then proceeded to tell the other four officers present all about my community outreach singing program.

"Seriously?" one of the officers said. "You were a singer before becoming a cop?" I smiled and shrugged. "Yeah, I was a country western singer." Officer Levan said, "Like a no kidding singer? With a cowboy hat and a guitar?" "Yep," I said, "the whole shebang."

Another officer in the back of the room stood, holding his hand over his radio mic to muffle the chatter. "Eric Moutsos, country superstar.""No," I said, "I wasn't that big, but I did work for the Real Deal.""What's the Real Deal?" someone said. I opened my mouth to reply, but my partner spoke first. "Not what. Who." "Huh?" the officer in the back said. My partner shook his head in disgust. "You don't know who the Real Deal is?"

A couple officers exchanged confused looks. "Evander Holyfield," my partner said. "You know, the boxer. Heavy-weight champion of the world." Comprehension filled the room, then everyone stared at me, expecting an explanation. "Okay, okay," I said. "I entered a regional country western contest called 'Nashville Star.' I did pretty good." "How good?" somebody asked. "Regional finalist," I said. "Holy crap, that ain't bad," an officer said. "How was it working with the Champ?" another officer asked.

I brightened at the memory. "Oh, he is the one of the great-est people I have ever, ever met." I sat on a table, resting my duty belt against a whiteboard. "How I met him was kind of a fluke, a chance meeting. Get this, my dad is at a training for his work and hears about how well I did on Nashville Star. In the middle of the class, my dad pipes up about the text he got, about how I did. Well, one of the other guys in the class just happens to be Evander Holyfield's friend. They start talking. The guy sets up a meeting between me and Evander. I had no idea the Champ had a record label, let alone an ear for country music. Next thing I know, I'm fly-ing to Atlanta to meet the Real Deal."

My brother grabbed my shoulders and gave me a shake. We stood in our parents' living room. He raised his voice, almost a scream. "You have got to take me. No way you are

going without me. No way." My brother had just learned
that I was about to fly to Atlanta to meet Evander Holyfield.
I considered teasing him, but his expression was so earnest I
could only smile and nod.

A part of me still couldn't believe this was happening. I'd
never been a serious performer. Only a year ago I was bored
out of my mind, living in my parent's basement, when I'd
done a search for country songs. I discovered a chatroom for
aspiring country musicians. People would take turns singing,
strumming their five-and-dime guitars, and bellowing into
cheap microphones. I was intrigued.And entertained.

A woman sang, "Stand by your man..." Another woman
sang a song I'd never heard, something about tractors. A
man sang, "How do you like me now," by Toby Keith. More
singing, one a little better, one a little worse. I always passed
whenever my turn came around. There were about thirty of
us, all from different cities, different backgrounds, different
beliefs, but loving the same music. We sat in front of our
computers, performing on our virtual stage.

I began to look forward to that part of my day, when I
would go down to the basement and open up this country
western chatroom. I didn't even own a guitar at the time. I
couldn't afford lessons. But for some bizarre reason, I just
knew something important was happening, that this was
somehow important for me to be a part of.

One day, I didn't pass. I pressed the spacebar and activated the microphone. A long pause. I felt a sudden panic. I could hear my rapid breathing coming back to my ears through the internet. Then someone started singing.

Looking back on the memory of
The dance we shared beneath the stars above

Who was singing? *I* was singing. I struggled to keep my throat from swelling shut with anxiety.

For a moment all the world was right
How could I have known that you'd ever say goodbye

Cheering. My eyes widened. I couldn't believe it. I didn't sound like Garth Brooks, but I wasn't half bad. I was as surprised as they were.

And now I'm glad I didn't know
The way it all would end
the way it all would go
Our lives are better left to chance
I could have missed the pain
But I'd have to miss the dance

The cheering continued. I grinned and continued to sing.

The disembodied female voice filled the airport corridors, clearly heard over the chatter and movement of hundreds of people. "Passengers for Delta 1737 nonstop to Atlanta at Gate D8."

My brother grabbed my guitar and I grabbed our two bags. We were going. I still could hardly believe it. I grinned from ear-to-ear.We boarded, stowed our bags, and buckled in. The flight was smooth. A female flight attendant glanced down at my lap where I gripped a faded cowboy hat, then back up at me. She winked, then turned up the aisle to continue with the drink service.

"No ear jokes," I said to my brother, referring to Evander's mangled ear, a souvenir from his fight with Mike Tyson, when Tyson had infamously bit him.
"I'm not making any promises," my brother said. "I'm serious." I said. "So am I," he said, grinning.

I dozed in and out of sleep until the jet touched down on the wet runway. After a quick taxi to the gate, we grabbed our bags and the guitar. I put on my cowboy hat and became Eric Ryan. Eric Ryan was my stage name, Ryan being easier than Moutsos to pronounce and to remember.

We walked off of the jet bridge. I grabbed my cell phone and thumbed for the number I'd been given. "Hello," Evander Holyfield said. I blinked in surprise, mouth open, then remembered to speak. "Hi, it's Eric Moutsos. My brother and I have arrived." "Just come out front and I'll get you," Evander said. He hung up and I stood there staring at my phone. This experience was becoming less of a dream and more of a reality. I was about to meet the Champ. I felt giddy.

As we approached the curb, a black Escalade pulled up and parked. A stout man, muscled, as if he just stepped out of a ring, or could step into one at any moment, strode around the front of the Cadillac. Evander Holyfield stuck out his hand. I grinned and we shook. "It's good to see you, Mr. Holyfield." "All right, all right," he said. "Welcome to Atlanta."

Evander grabbed the guitar and walked it to the back of his car. I gawked, surprised that he didn't have "people" helping him. But that was Evander, hands on, a personal touch, something I came to admire about him.

On the freeway, riding shotgun, I found myself staring at his right ear. I sensed my brother watching and I looked over my shoulder. His eyes were bright, his lips pressed in a tight smile. Evander must have sensed what we were thinking. He said, "For thirty-five million, you can bite the other one."

My brother and I shared a look, hesitated for a moment, then laughed. I glanced up just in time to see a street sign that said, "Evander Holyfield Highway." We took a right, then arrived at a mansion so big it indeed needed its own street. "That's my highway," the Champ said.

I looked back at my brother again, both of our mouths hanging open."How much land does this property sit on?" I asked. "Let's go see," the Champ said, and pulled off the road to park on the immaculately manicured grass. He pointed. "It goes all the way to those trees over there, and back up that way to the pond. Two hundred and fifty acres." My brother and I exchanged amazed looks.

We exited his vehicle, grabbed our stuff, and followed Evander inside. I felt like I was entering a palace for royalty. "Right this way," the Champ said. The mansion was eerily quiet, no one else around.

Evander led us to a room off one of the wings of the mansion. This area looked lived in: clothes folded on a chair, a desk with a computer. "Okay," Evander said, "let's hear it." I looked up and blinked. "What? You mean, sing? Now?" Evander smiled and nodded. He sat on a big, plush chair. I gulped.

I placed the guitar case on the sofa, unhinged the clasps, and held my guitar. Only a year ago, I had picked up a guitar for the very first time. Nowhere I was, about to perform for THE Evander Holyfield. At his house! My future became this one moment. I strummed the guitar and breathed in and out, slow, steady.My voice filled the silent room. I sang an original.

> I felt the sun shine when I woke up this morning
> Dark clouds drifted by without warning

Evander's eyebrows lifted. He perked up for a moment, then relaxed back against his chair.

> And you were by my side and I felt warm inside
> I think I fell in love again

Evander stood. He walked into the adjoining room without saying a word, nodding his head as he went. I tossed a quizzical look in my brother's direction, then hurried after Evander. I followed the Champ through part of his maze-like, 28,000-square-foot mansion. I felt dazed. I'd flown 2,400 miles and had sung only four lines. What was happening?

I managed to stammer a few words. "What did you think?" Evander glanced over his shoulder. "I'm going to have some people get some papers to you." I stumbled, but caught myself before I fell. "Wait. So I got a record deal?""Yep," Evander said. "I want to help you."My brother slapped my back and we grinned like idiots.

A crazy idea tumbled into my thoughts: This would be a perfect time to show him our backyard boxing matches. I rummaged in the duffel bag that hung from my brother's shoulder. "What?" my brother said. "The video," I said. "What? Oh, right." From a side pocket, my brother yanked out a copy of the fights. "Mr. Holyfield," I said. "Yes." "I have an idea on how we can celebrate."

A brief explanation later, then a detour to a room with a giant television, and we were on a couch, sitting next to the man who beat Mike Tyson twice, watching my boxing match with Michael the Polynesian. I felt pathetic next to the Champ, but proud, too, like a kid who'd drawn a picture for his famous painter father.
Evander actually watched with genuine interest. Near the end of my fight, he raised his arms, like a boxer, his fists to either side of his head. "You've gotta keep your head up when you're fighting, Eric, and pick your punches. How you gonna know what you're swinging at if your head is down?"

In the years to come, those simple words of advice would have an enormous impact on me. Keep your head up. Pick your punches. How you gonna know what you're swinging at if your head is down?

CHAPTER 7

"Good parenting does not mean giving him a perfect life; it means teaching him how to live a good and happy life in an imperfect world."

—UNKNOWN.

Happy Birthday Robbery

I stood just inside the gas station convenience store. I shifted my weight and glass crunched beneath my boots. One of the other responding officers used his leg like a hockey stick to clear the main aisle of a handful of Doritos bags. A woman had backed into the display, knocking it over when the man in front of her started yelling at the clerk, demanding money and claiming to have a gun.

"I got this, Moutsos," the officer said. "Will you see if the witness statements are done?" I nodded and went outside. Two teenagers sat on the curb with clipboards on their laps. The Hispanic teenager looked bored, so I approached him first. "Hey, Miguel, you okay? "Yeah, I'm all right." "Are you finished with your witness statement?" He handed me the clipboard and attached witness statement, which detailed the robbery from his perspective.

"Got mine, too," the other teenager said, a blonde kid with eyebrows like caterpillars and a habit of chewing on his lower lip. "Thanks, guys," I said. "You need a ride home, or want to call your parents to get you?" Miguel patted his skateboard. "Naw, we live just up the street. Five minutes and we're home." "You sure?" I said. "It's getting dark." "Yeah, we're sure," Miguel said. He punched his friend's shoulder. "C'mon,man. Night's almost wasted."

I scanned their witness statements, nodded to them, and said, "Thanks for your help. Let the sergeant over there know you're ready to go." A woman began to sob, the third witness, the one who'd knocked over the Doritos display. She leaned against the convenience store wall, shuddering, hugging herself and squeezing her eyelids shut. I ducked back inside, grabbed a few napkins, then returned to the woman."Here," I said. The woman snatched the napkins, wiped her cheeks, and said, "I just wanted some snacks for our movie night." "I know," I said--she'd mentioned that multiple times. "What's happening to this world? I can't even get gummy worms without...without..."

The sobbing overtook her. I patted her shoulder and tried to soothe her. The Channel 4 and Fox13 news vans had arrived and were setting up.

My cell phone buzzed in my pocket. I slid it out just enough to see that the number belonged to my mother. I ignored it. I'd call her back when I had a minute. "Ma'am," I said. "Did you finish your statement?" She nodded, blew her nose, then stooped and grabbed her clipboard and statement. "Did you get ahold of your husband?" I said, and took the clipboard. "Yes, but I told him I'd drive home. I'll be fine to drive home. I will." My phone buzzed again. I glanced at the number. My mom. Maybe it was urgent.

I turned to the woman and said, "I'm sorry, I'll be right back." I wandered a few paces away, tucked the witness statements beneath an arm, and answered my phone. "Mom, can I call you back?" "I just need to know where you are." "What?" "Eric, where are you?" "Mom, I'm working. Now isn't a good time." "Well, just tell me where you are." "Mom, I--" "Honey, where are you?" I sighed and gave her my location. "Oh, okay. Love you, Eric." "Love you, Mom."

I shook my head, pocketed my phone, and went back to work. A few minutes later, while speaking to my sergeant, I noticed an older, white Buick creeping up alongside the gas station. The car turned and headed towards the crime scene. The slow speed and the fact that the headlights were off immediately caught my attention. I tensed, put a hand on my gun, thinking, *It's the robber coming back. It's a set up. It's...*

"Moutsos?" my sergeant said. "Are you listening? I...Hey. What the heck is that?" From the front passenger seat, tiny lights flickered. Were those...? I squeezed my eyes shut. "No, no, no," I muttered. "What, Moutsos?" my sergeant said. I opened one eye. Yep. The lady sitting on the passenger seat was none other than my mom. She held a cake. A birthday cake. *My* birthday cake.

Singing erupted from inside the car, muffled at first, then louder as the windows rolled down. "Happy birthday to you," my mom and dad sang. "Happy birthday to you..." I groaned. I wanted to shrink to the size of an ant and sneak away. Instead, I rushed to the Buick, determined to stop this insanity before any other officers noticed what was going on. I bent towards my mom and, in a tight, low voice said, "Mom. No. Are you serious right now? This place just got robbed." Mom grinned and tried to hand me the cake through the window.

I recoiled as if the flickering candles were lit sticks of TNT. "No," I said. "Go." Mom scowled, huffed, then said, "Fine. You just seemed kind of down the last time we saw you, so we wanted to surprise you. Cheer you up." "I'm surprised," I said. "I'm super cheered. You're very nice, but I'm working. You have to go." "Hey, son," Dad said, grinning, "we get you at a bad time?" I grimaced and made shooing motions.

Mom reached out and patted my forearm. "At least kiss your mother goodbye." She puckered her lips and leaned towards me. I danced from one foot to the other, but they just waited, smiling at me. I ducked down and gave her a quick kiss. "Go," I said. "Happy birthday, son," my dad said, then put the car in reverse and drifted back.

Mom's wave goodbye was a wiggling of fingers out the window. "We'll save you some cake for after work." I shook my head, exhaled a long, pent-up breath, turned, and found seven officers laughing at me and my birthday surprise. A giggle slipped past my mouth. Someone broke the silence with, "Dude, Moutsos, was that your mom?" Several officers erupted with laughter as I just stood there with my mouth open. "Happy birthday dear Moutsos," someone else said in a singsong voice. "Happy birthday to you."

I noticed the lieutenant's dour expression. I thought, *I'm dead. He's going to write me up for this.* The lieutenant's attention shifted. "Sergeant," he said, "a word please.""Back to work," our sergeant said, and strode to the lieutenant. I glanced at the looks on my coworkers' faces and knew I would never live this down. I sighed and thought, *That cake better be good.*

CHAPTER 8

"If the Devil is real, then God must be real, too."
—JACOB VARGAS

The 911 Hang Up Saved My Life

I sat in my patrol car, parked on the corner of 5th North and Elm Street. The poorer neighborhood had not aged gracefully, many homes showing a decay born of neglect: patchy, struggling lawns occasionally made uglier by random junk; flaking paint; weeds squirming up through multiple cracks in concrete driveways and sidewalks. I was alone tonight, waiting for a call from dispatch.

I glanced out my window, then down at an article on my phone. Reading was my attempt to relax during a moment of down time. I'd already chatted on the phone with Stacey and told my kids that when it was time, they'd better go to sleep for mommy or they'd be handcuffed and severely tickled.

At about 5:00 p.m., my radio chirped and a female dispatcher said, "Officer Moutsos, we had a 911 hang-up from a cell phone near you. Can you check on it?" She gave me the location. I flung my phone on the passenger seat and sighed. Time to waste some gas. Ninety-nine percent of 911 hang-ups were accidental dials, malfunctions, or a young kid playing on a phone. Still, you had to clear the call, just in case. Less than a minute later, I arrived at the location of the call. I frowned at the vacant lot. Apparently, a field of weeds had dialed 911. I double-checked my coordinates. Yep. I was at the epicenter of the 911 hang-up.

I squinted and scanned my surroundings. I saw nothing amiss. Not far to my left, a man smoked on his porch. A bit farther to my right, a teenage girl watched her dog pee in the front yard. I grabbed my door handle, about to exit my vehicle to investigate further, when a triple beep emergency crossed my radio. I jerked ramrod straight, froze, and held my breath.

Dispatch said, "Shots fired at 5th North and Elm Street." I flinched and thought, *Holy crap, I was just there.* Dispatch continued, "Suspect is reported to have shot two people and is running north on Elm Street."

I hit my lights and sirens and stomped the gas pedal. My tires screeched. I yanked a hard turn onto 5th North and barreled towards Elm Street. A man, in the road, ran in my direction. My lights and sirens were on. Why was he charging me? My eyes widened. He's the guy. The suspect. Shooter. I stomped the brake and jerked to a stop, shoved my door open, and jumped out. The man was a little over thirty yards away. My gaze jerked to his hands. They appeared empty. But he shot two people. He had to be armed.

I yanked my gun up and took a shooter's stance behind my open car door."Stop!" I yelled. "Police! Stop!" The man kept coming. "Police! Get on the ground! Police!" My hand squeezed the grip of my gun. My index finger probed the trigger.The man twitched like a puppet yanked by a string tied to its left shoulder.

He slowed, then stopped about fifteen yards away. I could hear him panting. It sounded more like wheezing laughter. I gestured with my gun. "Get on the ground. Lay down on your stomach." The man--he was young--just stared. He didn't seem to blink. His eyes... There was something not right about him on a deeper level.
I swallowed. I tried to slow my breathing, tried to keep my gun steady. "Get on the ground. Do it. Now." The man shivered. He made a bizarre noise, like someone imitating the sound of vomiting. "Get on the ground," I said. "Get on your stomach." The young man plopped down on the street. He rocked forward and lay on his belly.

Multiple sirens approached from different directions. My gun fixed on the suspect's center mass, I crept around the door to get a little closer for a better shot if it came to that.

His head was turned in my direction. Those eyes. What was wrong with his eyes? "The voices told me to do it," he said, talking fast and way louder than necessary. "They told me to do it. To do it. I said I didn't want to but I wanted to. You know? They told me to do it. Do it. Do it. Do it."

A police car stopped behind me and a car door opened and slammed."Hey." A man's voice. "Is that him? That's the suspect?" I nodded, but kept my attention on the young man on the ground. "Yeah," I said, surprised that my voice sounded so steady when inside, my heart pounded a wild, staccato beat against my ribs. A third car arrived. "I'll cuff him," the officer said. "Cover me."

The officer, who I now recognized, approached the suspect at an angle. He holstered his weapon, grabbed the young man's wrist and pulled the arm back, handcuffing one wrist, then the other. I glanced farther up the street. A handful of people gathered around a body sprawled on the grass in the front yard of a brick house.

"Hey," I said, "someone's hurt up there. You got him?" The officer nodded as he patted the suspect, searching for weapons. I holstered my gun and sprinted south on Grant Street. I approached the people in the yard. A middle-aged male in shorts, a t-shirt, and only one flip-flop slumped on his side, a hole in his head, the grass beneath sticky and dark with congealing blood. His eyes were open, but unfocused and glassy. Definitely dead.

More officers arrived. Farther ahead, more people. Another body? I ran, hoping the next victim was alive. CPR and first aid swirled through my thoughts. Three other officers reached the body before me. I slowed to a brisk walk, catching my breath. People backed away from the officers, making room, but huddling together, whispering and gesturing. The officers inspected the body of a young man in jeans and a baseball style shirt, maybe the same age as the suspect.

I blinked at my surroundings. *No,* I thought. *No way.* I took a step back.This was the corner where I'd been parked before the 911 hang-up. I'd been right over there just minutes ago. In my mind's eye, I saw myself sitting in my car, reading, a figure with a gun creeping up behind and... I gave my head a shake. *Don't think about that. There's work to do.* I approached the nearest bystander, an elderly man in shorts and a white tank-top that displayed a prodigious amount of curly white chest hair.

"Do you know what happened?" I said. "That lunatic shot his friend here in the back. In the head." A black lady, gripping the elderly man's arm, peeked around his shoulder and said, "I knew something like this was bound to happen. All that kid ever did was play video games and sell drugs. You ask Anna Sanchez. She'll tell you." "Did you see the shooting?" I asked. The man shook his head. "Heard the shots and peeked out my window."He pointed across the street. "I live over there. Anyway, saw him running that way, his friend here on his knees, then plopping on his face."

Paramedics relieved the three officers who'd been performing CPR. The watch commander called me over and we discussed what I'd seen and done. Detectives arrived. Crime scene arrived. Photos taken. Evidence secured. A handgun was found. Casings by the bodies. More support staff arrived. News crews set up along the perimeter of the crime scene. Hours passed. Reports completed. Interviews.

My shift ended and it was time to go home. I opened my car door and bent to get in, but paused. I stared at the spot where I'd been parked before the murders began. The voices had told that young man to kill his friend. If I'd still been there, if there'd been no 911 hang-up, what would the voices have told him to do to an officer sitting alone in his car? I shivered, got in and drove.

Halfway home, tears blurred my vision and emotion burned my throat. It wasn't sadness. It wasn't fear or relief. It was undiluted gratitude. In my heart, I absolutely knew God had saved my life. The coincidence was just too great. I got dispatched to a 911 hang-up call – a nothing call, and it swept me away from a violent encounter that could have ended my life. I used to hate 911 hang up calls, they were so pointless. But I believe this one saved me. I owed God. I owed Him more than ever. I re-committed to serving Him,

being a better father, a better husband, a better cop.
Just...better.

   I offered a prayer of thanks. I was so blessed. I parked in
my driveway. I drew a deep breath, held it a moment, then
exhaled and rubbed my face. "Thank you for my home," I
whispered to God. I crept upstairs to my bedroom. Stacey
lay in bed. With my toes, I shoved one boot off, then the
other. I always stripped my gear and changed out of my uniform as soon as I could, but this time, I just laid down
alongside my wife and clung to her body. "Honey," Stacey
said. "What? You're still dressed." Voice cracking, I told her
what happened.

CHAPTER 9

Paralyzing Fear

"What did I do?" the fifty-something-year-old homeless man said in a reedy, slurred voice. He resembled Jafar from Disney's *Aladdin,* when Jafar dressed up like the nutty old guy to trick Aladdin into retrieving the magic lamp. I realized that I was staring at his lack of teeth and the black rot of those few that remained. I gave my head a quick shake and met his bloodshot eyes.

"I told you," I said. "We've received multiple complaints about you." "Complaints?" His eyes bulged. "About me? Who would complain about me?" "You're intoxicated on a busy sidewalk, yelling obscenities at people, and you pushed a woman who wouldn't give you a dollar. Plus, you have a warrant. You're under arrest."

The homeless Jafar impersonator wheezed with slow motion laughter and pointed at me as if I'd got him good with a hilarious prank. Sighing, I led him by the arm to my car, supporting him so he wouldn't fall.I helped him into the rear seat, gagging when I got anywhere within range of his halitosis. We headed to the county jail.

Moments after pulling onto the freeway, a horrific stench punched me in the nose. I grimaced, then glared at the homeless guy in my rear-view mirror. Grinning, he said, "How's that for my right to remain silent?" "Are you freaking kidding me?" I rolled down my window and leaned towards the fresh air. Homeless Jafar cackled. "Don't do that again," I said. He ripped a loud, sputtering fart, clearly audible above the roar of wind through my open window.

I clenched my teeth and waited for the inevitable wall of stink. When it hit, I gagged. I dry heaved. I doubted I'd smelled anything worse in my life. I couldn't take it. I pulled over, jerked to a stop, yanked the key out of the ignition, and burst out of the car. I gulped fresh air with only a hint of car exhaust. Traffic rushed by at seventy miles per hour. Despite the cacophony of passing vehicles, I could hear his maniacal laughter from within the car. He yelled, "I got another one for when you come back. Gonna hold it until you get in." His face was red as a tomato from laughing so hard. I ground my teeth. I wanted to pull him from the car and kick the fart out of him. I squeezed my eyes shut and ordered myself to act professional. No matter how degenerate, he was still a human being. Eventually, I got back in and we headed to jail, front windows open.

As soon as I had left the jail and the homeless Jafar, the radio buzzed. Officers needed help. 10-78. Expedite. I didn't turn on my lights and sirens, but I sped onto 33rd South, heading back to the freeway, but breaking a few traffic policies to try to get to my comrades. A quick hop on the freeway and off at the off ramp and a last quick left.

There they were, just outside of the homeless shelter. Officers grappled with someone, what we called a "pig pile-up." I stomped on my brakes, tires screeching. I jumped out of my patrol car, dashed to my comrades, and joined the pile-up. My first thought was, *This isn't normal.* "Stay down!" I yelled at the man beneath us. "Quit fighting!" I leaned forward and tried to pin the man's right shoulder and head to the sidewalk.

The officer to my left cursed. The officer to my right panted and grunted and gushed sweat. The man on the ground convulsed, twisted, and heaved. He kicked and the officer holding the man's leg flew backwards. The officer rolled. He scrambled to his hands and feet, then dove again, snatching the man's leg and trying to pin it beneath his body again. Watching, I thought of Tarzan wrestling an anaconda.

The suspect appeared to be in his early forties. He could have been an extra in a vampire movie: pale skin; long, slick black hair; well-trimmed goatee. And strong. Freakishly strong. Yeah, like a vampire. The officer to my left shouted, "Stop resisting! Stop resisting!" My hands ached. My arms and shoulders burned. I yelled, "Stay down!" I thought, *He doesn't stink like most homeless guys.*

I gave my head a quick shake. What was I thinking about? His smell? The man laughed, a jerky sound full of dark amusement. "How many does it take to keep me down?" His amusement twisted, becoming rage. He roared.I nearly lost my grip. What was he on? Amphetamines? Five cops against one guy and we could barely keep him down. They'd kicked him out of the homeless shelter because he wouldn't stop screaming. Handcuffs finally ratcheted.

The man bellowed. He arched his back, bending taut like a bow pulled to launch an arrow, straining against his re-straints --straining, straining, then suddenly relaxed. The man squirmed halfheartedly. "Knock it off already," the officer on the left leg said. The man's shoulders shook with silent laughter. I realized his breathing was almost normal. Not ours. We gulped air and wheezed.

We rolled him onto his back and the man's gaze locked with mine. I felt a jolt inside my head and an invisible thump to my chest. The man's lips pulled back and twisted in a corrupted version of a smile. I shrugged, suddenly and overwhelmingly uncomfortable.

Those eyes. They weren't just dark. They were pits, and I sensed something lurking down in those depths, something infinitely sinister. I wanted to turn my head, but couldn't. I had to break this bizarre spell, so I said, "What's your problem?" The man glanced at my nametag. He licked his lips and his eyes returned to my face. He said, "What's *your* problem, Moutsos?"

His perfect pronunciation of my last name and the familiarity in his voice startled me. Nobody get my last name right. I pulled back as far as I could without breaking my hold on his shoulder. Slowly, we drew back, but remained ready to re-engage the man if he started to fight. We hauled him to his feet. "Moutsos," someone said. I turned. Our sergeant exited his vehicle and strode toward us. I nodded a greeting.

"What is this?" I glanced over my shoulder. One officer held the man's right arm, another officer held the left. They searched him for weapons and anything else he shouldn't have. I explained the situation to our sergeant. As I spoke, I noticed the man watching me from about twenty feet away. He did not occasionally glance in my direction, but stared intently, black eyes glittering. His attention made the hairs of my arms and the base of my neck stand on end. Goose-bumps. His lips were moving. I realized he was saying my name, over and over, just loud enough that if I stopped talking I could hear, but not loud enough that the officers searching him would be so annoyed that they'd order him to shut up.

"Moutsos. Moutsos. Moutsos..." "All right then," our sergeant said, and nodded in satisfaction. "Moutsos. Moutsos. Moutsos..." "Book him into jail." I blinked at our sergeant. "Me?" I said. "Sure," our sergeant said. "Get this wacko booked." "Moutsos. Moutsos. Moutsos..."

I grimaced and considered asking if he'd have somebody else take the man to jail. "Moutsos. Moutsos. Moutsos..." *Don't be a wuss,* I silently told myself. "Moutsos. Moutsos. Moutsos..." I headed for my patrol car. Halfway there, I glanced over my shoulder. The man's head was slightly bowed, but he peered up at me from beneath his slim, black eyebrows. His lips still moved with the shape of my last name. My stomach twisted. I thought, *He's possessed. He's full-on demonic.*

I noticed that we had drawn an audience of homeless people a short way up the street, closer to the entrance of the shelter. The rest of the way to my car, I felt watched, eyes drilling into the space between my shoulders. I told myself not to let my imagination run wild. He was just a man. But that strength? And that...that darkness inside and around him? Was that darkness my imagination, too?

I started my car, then arced around to the other side of the street, parking near my partners, our sergeant, and the bizarre vampire-man. The arrestee's body language was calm, but a weirdly pleased smile had slithered onto his face. He stared ahead, looking at nothing. I lifted my chin, clenched my teeth, and exited my car. This man would not scare me. Look at him. He's handcuffed. He's deflated. Defeated.

I swung out of my car and walked toward the man and the officers who held him. Vampire-man's head slowly turned in my direction. His gaze locked on mine. He smiled, licked his, lips and said, "Moutsos is back." I scowled and stood straight, but inside I squirmed.

I seized the man's elbow and yanked him away from my partners. I did a quick search, patting him down, but found no weapons or drugs. I doubted I would. If the guy had anything on him, my partners would've found it during their search. Still, it felt better to double check. I then escorted him to my patrol car, shoved him inside, and clicked the seat belt into place. I threw him a final glare for good measure, to let him know who was in charge here. I went to the driver's seat and ran his ID on the computer. No criminal record, just a few traffic infractions. That surprised me. I was certain he'd have something.

Into my radio, I said, "B-187, I'll be en route to jail with one from the shelter." "Copy, B-187," dispatch said. I headed towards the freeway. Out of habit, I turned on the radio, searching for a good tune to listen to while I drove. Nothing but commercials. I considered throwing on a CD, or an inspirational talk. I had an audiobook on my phone. Maybe I'd-- Click. I glanced up at my rearview mirror.

He now sat on the middle of the back seat, leaning forward, his face hovering an inch away from the cage that separated the rear of the cab from the front. The click had been his seat belt releasing.

"Moutsos," he said, "I know who you are." A chill wriggled along my spine. Unwilling to show fear, I snorted and said, "What do you mean, who I am?" My voice trembled slightly, betraying my outward bravado. "You know nothing about me." "What does the 'E' on your name-tag stand for?" he said, grinning, eyes glittering, not with mirth, but like the eyes of a snake, simply reflecting light. I glanced down at my name-tag. I opened my mouth to reply, but he spoke first.

"Hello, Eric. It is Eric, isn't it, Eric?" I tried to hide my surprise by changing lanes. "Eric Moutsos," he said, perfectly, and chuckled softly. My face felt cold. My heart beat too fast. I had the urge to slam on my brakes so his face would smack the cage. Instead, I picked up my phone, deciding to distract myself by calling my wife. No answer.

The man said, "Everyone knows who you really are, Eric. You aren't fooling anyone. I know your sins. Everyone sees through you, just like me. Those naughty thoughts you think. What if your family knew? They'll see you for who you are as they get older, as they learn more about how this world works, and how daddy's mind works. Yes, Eric, they'll see how big of a fraud you are. They'll figure out what you've done when you were younger. Those were wild years, weren't they, Eric?"

Fear paralyzed me. He continued, getting specific about some of the things I'd done in my past, before coming back to church, before Stacey and our marriage. Was he guessing because everyone has a past, or did he actually know my exact sins? I felt like I was pinned down.

I stared at this man, this stranger. I wanted to scream at him, deny everything he said, but I couldn't speak. I couldn't speak, so I prayed in my heart, and the thought came to play some spiritual music. I fumbled for my iPod and turned on a church hymn. He laughed. I turned up the volume. He laughed louder. I pressed my foot down on the gas pedal. I wanted him gone, booked into jail and gone.

He raised his voice to be heard above the music. "You'll never be forgiven for those things. God doesn't forgive a faker." I started praying in my heart. Please, God, please, make this stop. The man shrieked and snarled. "Fake! Your children will grow up to call you cursed! Cursed and fake!"

I turned onto jail property. The man's foul words assaulted my ears. I announced myself to the jail and entered the booking area parking lot. I parked. I turned off my engine. I removed my seatbelt. In a quiet voice, my prisoner said, "I'll always be watching you, Eric. I'll make sure you're fake." I exited the car. The man said nothing more. He followed every order.I booked him in and fled the jail. I went home. I didn't sleep. Who could sleep after a conversation with the devil?

CHAPTER 10

*"**Embarrassment** is an emotional state that is associated with moderate to high levels of discomfort. Usually some perception of loss of honor or dignity (or other high-value ideals) is involved, but the embarrassment level and the type depends on the situation."*

—WIKIPEDIA

The Cookie

I examined the cookie that all other cookies aspired to.

Oversized. Chunks of chocolate. Still warm. I broke a piece off. Gooey. Moist. I popped it into my mouth, chewed slowly, and savored. The cookie compelled me to halt in front of our substation exit. I didn't think a cookie had ever made me stop in my tracks before. This was that good.

Our family budget only allowed for around $20 cash for me to eat out each month. Dollar menu items mainly. Sure, I could make a PB&J, but it sometimes got old. Many don't know this sad truth, but when we started as police officers in Salt Lake City, most of us qualified for food stamps under the pay we received. Other agencies in the state paid even less. I didn't know how they made ends meet.

On Rio Grande Street where the homeless shelter was, there were days when I would watch people bring the homeless food. Lots of food. Sometimes salivating over it. Hot meals. Hamburgers, hotdogs, Kentucky Fried Chicken, you name it. Three times a day, every day. There were days I wanted to put on shaggy clothes and dress up like a homeless person, just to go eat a great meal.

Leaving the substation, I crossed the parking lot to my police car, wishing I'd gotten a second cookie. I turned my key, then cranked the A/C, mentally commanding the cold air to hurry up and save me from this sweltering summer afternoon. Wearing a bulletproof vest never helped the scorching desert heat in Utah. I headed out on patrol.

Some twenty minutes later, I was parked near the homeless shelter when a man with a graying beard and tinted glasses waved, trying to get my attention. I rolled down my passenger-side window. "Hi, officer," the man said. "I work near the homeless shelter. I thought you should know there's a group of men selling drugs. They're the ones near the kids' playground. About eight of them." I thanked the man and promised to investigate.

I drove around the corner, parked, and exited my car. I found a group of men near the playground, as described. The group of men appeared to be in their forties, all huddled in a semicircle, fixated on what a man in the middle was holding. One of the men spotted me approaching. He stiffened and his eyes widened. His buddies noticed his reaction, then noticed me. They inched away from the man in the middle, everyone trying to look casual. Somebody near the shelter entrance yelled, "Busted!" then barked a laugh. The man in the middle stood. He leaned against the fence and did an impressive job at looking bored and unconcerned.

I approached the man, believing that they had to be doing something illicit.They certainly weren't trading baseball cards. I glanced at the children scampering around the playground on the other side of the metal fence, then scowled at the man. "Sir, sit on the curb. Don't move. Don't talk to anyone." I turned, intending to interview one of the men who'd been in the semi-circle, when the man in the middle spoke. "Why I gotta sit here?"

I rounded on the guy, my voice a bit harsher than I'd intended, but drug deals near children don't make me happy. I jabbed a finger in his direction. "Just sit there and don't talk until I come back." He paused, peering at me with his head cocked to one side, then busted up with laughter. My cheeks heated. I narrowed my eyes.

My lips tightened. I said, "Do not mess with me right now." To my bewilderment, he laughed harder. He gestured at me and a few of his nearby companions grinned or joined in the laughter. *They must be high*, I thought. I planted my fists on my hips and hurled my best you morons are messing with the wrong guy expression.

I separated and interviewed each man who'd been in the semi-circle. Their independent stories matched. I couldn't find any law that was broken. I felt cheated. I'd wanted so badly to pin them with something, especially for their disrespectful laughter. I returned to my car, shook my head one final time in disgust, then pulled into the street and drove past them.

The men slapped each other on the shoulders and sputtered with laughter. *They had to be high,* I thought, and glared at them in my rearview mirror. Then I noticed something odd, something on the tip of my nose. A big brown blob. "What?" I said. My eyes widened. The cookie. I had what looked like an entire chocolate chip glued to my nose.

I replayed my entire exchange with the men by the homeless shelter, this time from their perspective. I snorted and found myself chuckling with the men shrinking in my rearview mirror. I considered going back and apologizing for snapping at them when they'd laughed, but I was too embarrassed. Instead, I returned to the substation and told my partners what had happened.

"Moutsos," one officer said, "those dudes owned you." "No," another officer said, "that cookie owned you." Later, during a quiet moment near the end of my shift, I reflected on the chocolate chip nose incident. Wasn't that how we all were, judging people based not on what they saw, but only from our own narrow perspective? Moral lesson learned or not, I didn't show myself on that corner for at least a week.

CHAPTER 11

"The more corrupt the State, the more numerous the laws."
—TACITUS

In the Name of the Law

Our sergeant stood at the front of our small briefing room behind a table, conducting the usual line-up meeting that began all of our shifts. He said, "As we discussed last night, we'll rendezvous at Main Street and 200 South at sixteen-hundred hours. I want the riff-raff cleared before the evening rush. There's also a concert at the Gallivan Center tonight, so let's make sure that gets extra attention. There were a lot of complaints from people about aggressive panhandlers and a couple of public urinations. What was that last event? Craft City or something? Well, you know the drill."

I glanced at the clock and was about to stand and head out for my shift, but our sergeant held up a hand and said, "One more thing." For a moment, he squinted and studied something above our heads. He then resumed, saying, "Our citation numbers are decent, but a bit behind the other shifts, so let's see if we can get our numbers up. Two challenges. The first one of you to ticket someone selling items without a license gets two hours off."

I raised my eyebrows and perked up on my seat. It would be wonderful to surprise my family by getting off work early and spending an evening with them. As a newer officer, I didn't have a lot of vacation saved up. Our sergeant held up two fingers. "The second challenge for today will be the first person to pull over and ticket a blue Ford or a yellow Toyota. That will also earn you two hours."

The officer to my right sighed. I glanced over just in time to see him finish rolling his eyes. He was a veteran officer and, like most senior officers, these little incentive games annoyed him. *Well,* I thought, *that's good. If he's too jaded to want to play, I'll have a better chance at winning the time off.* Our sergeant dismissed us and we headed out on patrol.

Less than an hour later, I was driving along State Street, turned a corner, and there it was: jackpot. I parked and leapt out of my car. With a variety of businesses along the street, this stretch of sidewalk hosted a good amount of pedestrian traffic, the perfect place if you wanted to sell something to passersby. I smirked.

The Hispanic kid was probably thirteen years old. He wore a blue shirt with white stripes and a collar, khakis, and shiny black shoes. He stood beside a metal cooler with a handle and wheels, a cardboard sign propped against it, listing the prices for each item.

This was it. No one had called over the radio that they'd stopped a unlicensed vendor. No way this kid had a license. This was my two hours off. "Corns!" the kid yelled, with a hint of an accent. "Corns! Sweet corns! Da best horchata! Cold horchata!" A woman purchased a corn on a stick for each of her three children. I waited for her to pay then leave. "Corns!" the kid yelled. "Horcha..." The kid noticed me approaching. He flinched and his teeth snapped shut. He hunched and his body seemed to shrink while his clothes remained the same size.

I stopped and frowned down at his cooler. There didn't appear to be much ice. Wouldn't the horchata spoil in this heat without ice? It didn't take a food health inspector to know someone could get sick if those drinks soured. Looked a bit dirty inside, too. What appeared to be mayo and sugar, or perhaps salt, slathered the corn. Some kind of white sauce. Gross, I thought. Mayonnaise? On a hot day?

The kid managed a wobbly smile and said, "Sir? You like something?" I stared at the kid for a moment, then said, "You know it's illegal to sell food like this without a license, right?" The kid blinked at me. "Do you have a vendor's license?" He looked to his right, then at his cooler, then back at me. "You don't want a corn?"

I shook my head.

"I'm sorry, kid. This is illegal. You can't sell this stuff here." He shifted his weight and shrugged. "We need to get your parents down here." I dialed the number he gave me and asked his parents to come to our location. "I'm sorry," I said, "but I have to give you a ticket, and you'll have to take all his home." "Ticket?" the kid said, looking up, but not quite making eye contact. "Yes." I took out my ticket book and pen and scribbled.

"Let's clean this up," I said. "I go home." He looked at me. "We need to wait for your parents to get here." His parents arrived and I gave the paperwork to them. They packed up his belongings and left. I thought: *He'll be okay. This will be a good lesson on how to do things the right way,* doing my best to justify this in my mind. I watched them drive off, then rushed to my patrol car and shot a message to my sergeant. A few minutes later, my sergeant replied: "Congrats, Moutsos. You won. You got the time off. Nice work." I grinned and started planning how I'd surprise my family and what we'd do together.

I nodded at the other bike squad officers gathered on Main Street. We chatted amongst ourselves for a few minutes before our sergeant showed up in his car. He parked, sauntered over, and began giving out assignments. "Moutsos, Ruiz, Bradshaw, you're with me. Let's get to work."

The three of us followed our sergeant, who approached two men sitting on a bench beneath the shade of mature trees. The men appeared to be in their forties, both with scraggly beards. They wore dirty shirts and grimy jeans, one with sandals, one with shoes that might have been white in a previous life. The homeless often migrated from the homeless shelter to enjoy the cooler, shaded air between the towering buildings along this stretch of road. I'd seen them here often enough, and it always struck me how differently they acted.

Away from the crowded, often hostile atmosphere of the shelter, they were relaxed, smiled and laughed more. I couldn't blame them for choosing this area. I'd want to get away from the shelter, too. The problem was that many of them begged for money, urinated in public, or worse, and otherwise irritated surrounding business owners, their employees, and customers. So this particular afternoon, we'd come down and warn them against misbehaving. We'd encourage them to hang out closer to the homeless shelter where they could use the bathroom there, rather than in an alley or pestering a business to use their facilities.

The two men noticed our approach and their conversation ceased. They exchanged a look and their shoulders sagged. "Gentlemen," my sergeant said, nodding to them. "We know, we know," the man on the left said, and they stood, retrieved their belongings, and headed down the sidewalk. I found a gap-toothed lady snoring on a blanket at the mouth of an alley, one of her legs jutting out onto the sidewalk, waiting for the unwary to trip over her. She cuddled a beer can like a child would a teddy bear. I noticed she wore three shirts. I always found it baffling how some homeless would wear layers of clothing in heat like this. Sure, they didn't have a home with a closet or dresser, but that had to be un-comfortable.

I nudged the woman with my foot. She snorted and smacked her lips. I nudged her more vigorously. She blinked, red-rimmed brown eyes slightly unfocused and dis-oriented."Huh-what? What? Whaaat?!" She spoke in a too loud, strident voice that made my teeth ache. "Ma'am," I said. "I'm sorry, but you can't sleep here." "Oh. Cops." She sat up. "Okay. Right. Whatever. Okay." I heard two men ar-guing nearby. I turned back to the lady and said, "Pack up and move on, please."

I didn't wait for her response. I hurried in the direction of the argument. My sergeant stood in front of a man who sat on a bench built into a raised planter box full of struggling shrubs. The middle-aged man reminded me of Bill Murray, but with a broken nose and chubbier by about twenty pounds. "I don't have to leave," the chubby Bill Murray said. "This is a public place." "You need to leave," my sergeant said. "Now." "I done nothing wrong."

My sergeant pointed to the man's backpack in the planter box behind him. "That. Right there." My sergeant turned to me and gestured at the backpack."Moutsos, I want you to write this guy up for destroying city plants." I stiffened, blinked, and said, "City plants?" "Yeah," my sergeant said, and rounded on the man. "It's illegal to harm city plants." "What?" the chubby Bill Murray said. "You gotta be kidding."

My sergeant was not kidding. I remembered seeing that code. How could I forget such an odd law, thinking at the time that maybe somebody had cutdown a city tree or something, and then this law popped up in response. "How on Earth am I destroying city plants?" the man yelled. My sergeant pointed. "Your backpack is in a city planter box." "Yeah? So?" "So plants grow in planter boxes. Your backpack is hurting those bushes."

I got out my pen and wrote the chubby Bill Murray a ticket. The man huffed and complained. My sergeant folded his arms, glared, and said, "Next time, just do what we ask. Cooperation is always easier." Chubby Bill Murray stormed off. I imagined he'd toss the ticket in the nearest garbage, if not chuck it in the street. I snorted with black humor. If he did, I could ticket him for littering. In a way, it was kind of nice to have so many laws. If someone was being a jerk, you could almost always find something to cite him for. So many laws, I thought. So little time.

CHAPTER 12

"Define success on your own terms, achieve it by your own rules, and build a life YOU'RE proud to live."

—ANNE SWEENEY

Unanswered Prayers

Stacey and I had met not long after that first meeting with Evander and she stole my heart, time, and attention. For the most part. Even though she was very supportive, it was difficult to be newlyweds, expecting our first baby, and having me gone a lot. Stacey didn't ever go to Nashville with me and it was a challenge for both of us to have me try to straddle two different worlds. I was also on the phone constantly, trying to push forward with my career, and that bothered her. Not to mention the strain of worldly pressure.

During a meeting with one of the record label presidents, he suggested that they promote me as a single man. "But I'm happily married," I told him, turning my wedding band around on my finger. "I'd prefer to wear my wedding ring everywhere I go." "It's awfully shiny, though, and would be a distraction on stage," he responded, as casually as he could. "Tim McGraw wears his wedding ring on stage," I said. "Well Tim McGraw was single once and he's Tim McGraw. He can do what he wants. Besides, we can sell you better as a single man. Younger girls buy a lot of records!"

After that conversation, I knew that particular label wasn't the right fit for me. Maybe that president was just feeling me out to see what I'd be willing to do, but definitely wasn't going to "sell myself" without Stacey. On another label visit, Evander and I met with the producer of a smaller record label, a guy named Mike. This is the guy who had found Tim McGraw and Leanne Rhymes. I played one of my demos for him. "Eric, you're a star!" he said excitedly, after listening to my song.

We immediately started talking about doing a joint-venture deal with Evander and taking my career to the next level. I was thrilled! I called Stacey to tell her and she was excited, too, but for some reason it didn't feel completely right to either of us. Ava was so tiny and we weren't making any money during all of this. We were living on credit cards and barely making ends meet.

Regardless of any hesitation we felt, I was soon sitting in an office in Nashville with Evander and a bunch of music people, most of them associated with BMI, signing on with Real Deal Records. Everyone was excited and I was pretty sure I was on my way to being a star, just like that producer had told me.

When I came home from one of my Nashville trips, Stacey and I watched *Walk the Line*, the movie about Johnny Cash and his life. The movie depicts what happened to him, how fame and fortune caused a lot of pain, heartache, and destruction along the way. His life was a disaster in so many ways and, as we watched the movie, I had a moment where I could see myself as him. Almost like a vision, I could see Eric Ryan as Johnny Cash Part 2. I tried so hard to pretend that I didn't see it, but I did.

Almost NO relationship in the entertainment industry works out in the end, I thought to myself. *Why do I think I'd be any different?* As I was having these thoughts, but trying my best to brush them aside, I noticed that Stacey was crying. When we got home, she went into our bedroom and shut the door. I could hear her sobbing behind our locked door. I think she had seen that vision of what our life could be – or not be – just like I had. And it terrified her. It took awhile for her to be able to talk about it without crying, but one day we had a conversation that told me how she really felt about the whole thing.

"Is this really what you want?" she asked after I told her I thought I'd better make another trip to Nashville. "Yes," I responded enthusiastically, almost angrily. "I believe that we can have a good life if I make it big. Once I start performing in front of thousands of people, making thousands of dollars, all our problems will go away." "But what if they get worse?" she asked. "What if it doesn't work out?"

I knew she had good points, but I didn't want to admit that she was right.I kept trying to make music work, justifying the choice in my mind by telling myself that the music industry would be good for us, that I could make it if I just pushed hard enough. But my conscience was screaming at me to run as faraway from Nashville as I could.

One afternoon, my cell phone rang and I saw that it was Mike from Nashville. "Eric, we need to do a radio show tour as soon as possible. Your record is fantastic and we need to push it right away!" I could see Ava and Stacey playing in the next room and couldn't help but feel distracted. "We want you to fly out next week," Mike told me. In that moment, God spoke to me and I knew, without any justification, what I had to do. I took a breath. "I'm sorry, but that's my daughter's 1st birthday," I said. "I can't come out that day." There was silence on the phone for several seconds, but it felt like an eternity. Finally, Mike said, "Eric, I don't think you understand what this is going to take." "I think you're right," I said. "I need to think about things."

I hung up and walked over to Stacey and Ava, dropping on the floor and breaking down crying. I knew it was over, but God comforted me in that moment. I had peace for the first time in a long time. Within a year, I entered the police academy. It was hard to leave my music dreams behind, but I never looked back. I knew God wanted that chapter to be closed and the next one to be opened. Looking back, there are times I got so mad at Stacey and other family members who voiced fears about me being part of the music industry. But now I know I was only getting mad because I was wrong the entire time and too afraid to admit it. Music life was not for us. It wasn't a life for my family. At least not at that moment in time. I think Garth Brooks was right when he sang about Unanswered Prayers.

CHAPTER 13

"Perspective is the way we see things when we look at them from a certain distance and it allows us to appreciate their true value."

—RAFAEL E. PINO

New Perspective

During my time on bike patrol, I gave Debbie about as many tickets as she had tattoos, which was a heckuva lot. And I wasn't the only one killing forests to issue all the tickets she received. Debbie was about fifty years old, barely over five feet tall, white beneath all that ink, with strawberry hair. And drunk. Almost always drunk. A chronic downtown nuisance, she was inevitably irritating someone, usually trespassing somewhere. I often thought, *if she'd saved all the money she spent over the decades on tattoos and booze, she might've bought a house by now.* Instead, she was homeless.

One evening, I responded to a call asking for help with a pan handler outside a bar and grill. Apparently, some lady

was harassing people in line, threatening, yelling, cursing, and urinating around the corner, but in view of anyone walking by. I neared the bar and coasted to a stop on my bike. About eight people waited to go inside. I then noticed who the panhandler was and groaned.Debbie. Again.
I set my bike aside and approaching her, threw up my hands. "Seriously,Debbie? Public intox? Public urination? Harassing people?" "I'm not doin' anything," she said, voice louder than necessary and a bit slurred. "Just sittin' here." "You're obviously drunk," I said. "The owner of the--""He don't own this sidewalk." "No, but you--" "You just go arrest a real bad guy, Mr. Law Man."

I pulled in a deep breath, closed my eyes, and exhaled. I said, "You can't be harassing people or leaving puddles of urine on--" "You're not in charge of me." I raised my voice to talk over her constant interruptions. "Don't you have anything better to do?" Debbie sneered at me. "Yeah? Same to you, Moutsos." "I have lots to do," I said in a tight voice. "But I have to deal with stupid people like you instead." Debbie cursed and called me some very impressive names.

I raised my voice and yelled over her, "This is what your life has come to,Debbie. Congratulations. Perpetually drunk and pissing in front of strangers. You're a real winner, Debbie. A real winner." Something I said, or perhaps the tone of my voice, affected Debbie. She flinched like someone had slipped an ice cube down her back. She blinked at me, expression horrified. Then her eyes turned shiny with accumulating tears that quickly spilled over onto her leathery cheeks. I sighed. I shouldn't have been so harsh. Just give her a ticket, make her move on, and leave it at that.

Debbie grabbed a water bottle with no label and shoved it into her faded, scuffed backpack with one broken strap. She grabbed some papers, a plastic bowl and a few other items, and jammed them in various pockets of the backpack. She stood halfway, turning left then right, lifting up her backpack and setting it down again three times.

"Where's my Bible?" Debbie said, a note of alarm in her voice "Where is it?" She whimpered and tugged snarly fistfuls of her hair. I frowned at the area around Debbie, but didn't see a Bible. Debbie plopped down on her butt, hung her head, and rocked forward and back. "My Bible. My Bible. I lost my Bible." I loomed over her, softened my voice, and said, "How did you get to this point, Debbie?" She stopped rocking, but didn't look up. I thought maybe she was too drunk to understand what I said, but she eventually spoke, so quiet that I had to lean closer to hear. "I used to have it all. They were so beautiful, those three little angels. My husband was good to me. Had a great job, too. It was all heaven...until it wasn't." I hunkered down beside her. "What happened?"

Debbie stared straight ahead, her body suddenly very still. "They just didn't come home, my husband and three of my four kids. Just never came home. Traffic accident. All four died instantly. Bam. Dead. Gone. Forever. Just me and one daughter left behind. Couldn't God take all or none of us? I just kept thinkin' that." My throat constricted and I turned away. I didn't want Debbie to see the sudden, unexpected pain in my expression. After all, I was a tough cop, not a bleeding heart social worker.

I studied a cluster of ragged people gathered a way up the street on the corner near the homeless shelter. I wondered how many carried a story like this. Some life-shattering tragedy that they couldn't cope with, a wound too deep to heal right. God must weep over these children. I certainly was now, tears stinging my eyes. I didn't know why this had struck me so hard, how this moment found a crack in my emotional armor and exploited it.

Debbie stumbled away in the direction of the shelter. I shuffled to my bike and took one last look at Debbie's shrinking form. I mounted my bike and peddled. I didn't have the heart to write any more tickets that night. I just sat on a park bench, pondering, praying silently, wondering what I could do for Debbie.

The idea of buying her a new Bible recurred, but, each time, I dismissed it with the excuse that I worked for government. Shouldn't mix church and state. Right? I remembered something I'd read not long ago. James Garfield had baptized over thirty people in one weekend when he'd been President of the United States. Well, if the president can baptize nearly three dozen people at a time, I could buy one person a Bible. I was just making excuses because what if she laughed in my face? Plus, something like this would embarrass me, especially if any of my fellow officers found out. I'd be teased to no end. *Well,* I thought, *suck it up, Eric. This is what God would want you to do.*

The next day, near the start of my shift, I ducked into a store and boughtDebbie a new set of scriptures. I even had her name embossed in golden letters on the bottom of the front cover. My ticket goals for the day faded to the background as I focused on trying to locate Debbie. She usually camped out somewhere in the open, so I drove my cruiser up and down the streets that she frequented. I circled Pioneer Parka half dozen times.

One hour became two; two became three. I finally resorted to asking for help. With a growl, I snatched my car radio and asked if anyone had seen the infamous Debbie, but nobody had a location for her. After my dinner break, I received a call over the squad radio. Someone had located Debbie. In the background of the radio transmission, I could hear her yelling. I smiled wryly and shook my head. It seemed she was getting another ticket.

My smile faded, replaced by determination. I had to get there quick. Debbie always stormed off after she got a ticket and the sun was setting. Night would make finding her even harder. I knew I shouldn't speed without a compelling reason. The public might complain and, in this case at least, rightfully so. I wondered what people would think if they knew a cop was speeding in an attempt to give a homeless woman a Bible.

I spotted the officer and Debbie. I pulled over alongside the officer's bike, hopped out, and rushed around the car, a plastic bag clutched in my right fist. Debbie spotted me and glared. "Oh, great. He's here." I held up the plastic bag. "What the hell is that?" Debbie said. "Gonna swing it? Hit me in the head? Beat up some more on poor Debbie.""Open it," I said. Debbie's eyes narrowed. "What is it?""Just take it and see."

Debbie looked from me to the confused officer, then back to me. She said,"What? I get a ticket and a present? Is that how it goes now? Who are...?" Her voice trailed off as she held the Bible up in front of her face. She squinted at her name embossed at the bottom. Her eyes widened and her mouth hung open. With each blink, her eyes grew wetter. She hugged the book to her chest, hunched protectively over it as she trembled and sobbed.

Despite the officer beside me, I choked up a bit, too. I sniffled, cleared my throat, then gestured clumsily at the Bible. "I marked a few things. Just some stuff that I like. You know how--" Her hug cut me off. She was bony, but surprisingly strong. "Thank you.Thank you. Thank you."

The officer beside me said, "So, um..." I flinched, remembering that I wasn't alone here. "Hey," he said to Debbie, "don't worry about that ticket." He glanced at me, then back to Debbie. "I won't turn it in. Just try to stay out of trouble. Okay?" The officer slapped my shoulder and headed to his bike.

When Debbie ended her embrace and stepped back, something went with her: a hardness to my heart that I hadn't realized was there. These people who broke the law, yeah, they did wrong, but they were still my brothers and sisters, still worthy of respect and love. Could I give a ticket to someone I cared about? I supposed I could, but it wouldn't be the same. There wouldn't be spite attached to it. There wouldn't be disdain and a sense of my superiority over the offender. I would do my job, but I wouldn't do it angrily. I would remember that I served the community -- all of the community. Even a chronic pain in the butt like Debbie, who taught me one of the greatest lessons of my life about perspective.

CHAPTER 14

"There is a higher court than courts of justice and that is the court of conscience. It supersedes all other courts."

—MAHATMA GANDHI

Strict Justice

My partner turned onto S. Rio Grande Street. I pointed to a spot just beyond the homeless shelter and said, "There's the van and the parking enforcement officer." My partner nodded. We'd been called to assist in a dispute between a parking enforcement officer and a man with multiple parking tickets whose van was to be impounded until the fines were paid. We passed the van, pulled over, and exited our car.

Rust peeked through the van's white paint; a hubcap was missing. On the sidewalk beside the van, a scruffy, middle-aged man stood, waving his arms, one moment pleading with the female parking enforcement officer, the next moment yelling. Great, I thought. Let's get this junk on wheels off the street so we can get to a real call. "C'mon," the van owner said. "It's all I got."

The parking enforcement officer noticed my partner and me, nodded to us, then smirked at the soon-to-be vanless transient. "Doesn't matter," she said. "The law is the law. You just had to keep parking illegally, again and again. You have so many unpaid fines that this is what happens. Follow the rules next time. Simple as that."

The man pressed his hands to his head and made a high-pitched shriek."We're at the homeless shelter. I don't have a place to park. The homeless shelter doesn't have parking for people staying here. Man, I got a job lined up, but I have to have the van to get there. Please. Just give me a little time. I promise, I'll pay." "I'll allow you to get your belongings from the van," the enforcement officer said. "You want to argue..." She gestured at my partner and me. "These two gentlemen can restrain you, or take you to jail for resisting or obstructing. Your choice."

The man faced us, gawked, and blinked with red-rimmed eyes. He whimpered, then spun and stomped to the side of the van, muttering to himself. He yanked the sliding side door open and ducked inside. The van bounced with his movements. The owner stumbled out carrying two car seats. He set them on the sidewalk, then went back inside. I glanced sideways at my partner who watched the unfolding scene in silence, studying every move.

The van owner continued to mutter and glower at the parking enforcement officer, though an occasional whimper broke through his anger, accompanied by a pained scrunching of his features. After his third trip to the van, tears began to streak his cheeks and glistened in his short beard. "Wasn't my fault I lost my job," he said. "Then I lose my house. Of course I lose my house."

Probably did drugs or showed up to work drunk. My mind focused on a profile I had created for this man. *You have to obey the law, pay your parking tickets just like everybody else,* I thought to myself. *Everybody has an excuse, but the law is the law.* The man entered the van, then exited with two booster seats for older children, which he set beside the car seats. Next came a duffel bag and two backpacks. As he removed items from the van, he kept glancing at a frumpy, middle-aged brunette and her four children, gathered about twenty yards away. I realized they must be his family.

The woman hugged herself and appeared to have tasted something sour. The two older children, a boy and a girl, somewhere around ten and eight, watched with wide, hardly blinking eyes. A boy of about five sat on the ground playing with a Hot Wheels car while a toddler squatted, staring intently at something on the sidewalk, maybe a bug. *Oh,* I thought, and shifted my weight from one foot to the other. *Great. They've dragged their kids into this homelessness. It's like a disease. What a mess.*

The man paused with a rolled-up sleeping bag in each hand. He turned to the enforcement officer, who watched with one eyebrow cocked and her lipsticked mouth pursed. "Please." He hefted the sleeping bags. "All our stuff, just sitting here on the sidewalk, by the shelter...They'll steal it. They only allow a few personal possessions inside the shelter. Please, it's all we have left." A tow truck arrived and the enforcement officer's face lit up like she'd seen an old friend. She waved the truck over.

"Please," the man said again to the enforcement officer, and then a whisper. "Please." "It's the law," she said, not looking at him. "It's the law." I grimaced and wondered if I ever looked so gleefully sadistic when I told somebody that I'd arrested, or cited, that it was "the law" and there was no use arguing. But, then again, the tow truck was already there. And like the lady said, it's the law. "Take it off!" someone yelled. I flinched, then realized the man who'd yelled was my partner. He'd been so quiet. I'd almost forgotten he was here.

The enforcement officer jabbed buttons on her phone, then sneered at my partner while she waited for someone to answer. When she spoke into her phone, her sweet voice did not match her expression. My partner had his own phone out and was making a call. I groaned. Parking enforcement versus Salt Lake PD? This couldn't end well.

Phone to his ear, my partner wandered over to our car and leaned against the door. A minute or so later, his call ended. He folded his arms and waited. I hurried to my partner. His poker face revealed nothing. "What's going on?" I said. He glanced at me, then over my shoulder at the enforcement officer, who paced as she spoke into her phone. My partner's attention returned to me. He said, "I talked to our sergeant, briefed him, and he's trying to get ahold of the lieutenant." The van owner stood beside his wife, rubbing her shoulder while eyeing us warily.

My partner's phone rang and he answered. "Yes. Uh-huh. Yeah, that's right. That's what I said." I listened to my partner's side of the conversation, but couldn't tell what was going on. I noticed the enforcement officer glaring at us. She flinched and brought her phone back up to her ear. She resumed her angry pacing, then stopped abruptly, spun to face my partner, and her eyes widened. She yanked the phone from her ear, stuffed it in her pocket, and stomped over to the tow-truck driver, who stood on the street beside his open door, his expression bewildered. Whatever she said, the tow-truck driver shrugged and headed for the back of his truck. He began to unhook the van.

I raised my eyebrows and grunted. *Wow*, I thought, and glanced at my partner, whose lips curved with a hint of a smile. The enforcement officer shot my partner with one of the most venomous looks I'd ever seen. The van owner and his wife stared silently at us, then at each other, then back at us. The enforcement officer slammed her door shut, window open, jabbed a finger in our direction and yelled, "When you guys go off duty, I'll find that van. I'll impound it. So you just wipe that look off your faces."

I shook my head and said, "What in the world just happened?" My partner shrugged. "Our boss talked to her boss. They agreed with my assessment." "Hey," the tow truck driver said, raising his hand like a student in a class."Who's paying for my time?" My partner approached the tow truck, sliding his wallet out of his back pocket as he went. He handed something to the truck driver.

My mouth opened as I realized my partner had just paid the driver with his own money. My partner and the driver shook hands. A moment later, the tow truck rumbled away. I felt small. Cowardly. I also felt a lot of respect and admiration for my partner. He'd gone out on a limb and done what he thought was right despite the risk involved to his career. "Hey," I said to my partner. "I have an idea."

"What's that?" I had just done a mental and philosophical about-face and wanted to follow his lead. "This is all for nothing if that van keeps parking illegally, right?" "Okay," my partner said slowly. I had his full attention now.

I grinned, though I wasn't sure if my plan would work. I did a search on my phone and found the number for a nearby hotel. I knew the manager pretty well, having answered several calls on his behalf. The receptionist forwarded my call and the manager answered. I then raced over to the hotel and explained the situation.

"So," I said to the manager, "if they could park their van on your lot for a little while, it won't be towed." The manager laughed. "You guys owe me." I thanked him and ran out. "We're good?" my partner asked. "We're good," I said. I jogged over to the waiting van owner and his family. I out-lined the plan. The man kept shaking his head and murmur-ing, "I can't believe it." The wife bit her lower lip and wept. When I finished talking, the couple took turns hugging my partner and me.We helped put their stuff back in the van and they drove away with a honk and a wave. My partner slapped my shoulder, "I guess we're done here." I nodded and we returned to our car.

Later, on my way home, my thoughts returned to my expe-rience with the van. My partner had seen how mercy could intervene with justice, and he had the integrity and courage to act according to his conscience. That parking enforcement officer could have impounded the van and been justified by the law, but just because something was legal, didn't always make it the best course of action. Something I'd recently read, something Abraham Lincoln had said, came to my mind: "I have always found that mercy bears richer fruits than strict justice."

I'd try to remember that as I continued in my career in law enforcement. There was something else that I tried to commit to: No matter what happened on the job, or in life, I had to try to follow the dictates of my conscience. Some days I would listen. Some days I would fail. I had to try to have the moral fortitude to act on what I believed to be right. I didn't know it then, but eventually, I'd discover just how much trouble a person could get in for doing what he or she thought was right.

CHAPTER 15

"We believe quotas create unnecessary tension between the public and law enforcement ... Quotas turn police officers into tax collection machines instead of professional law enforcement officers."
—THE ILLINOIS FRATERNAL ORDER OF POLICE LABOR COUNCIL

Turning Point

"Sorry, man," I said. "It's my job." The twenty-something-year-old man's brown eyes bulged; his mouth hung open. He wore a polo style shirt with the name of the shop where he worked. "But..." he finally said. "But I just spit on the sidewalk. That's all I did.""Right," I said, "and that's against the law." He barked an incredulous laugh, shook his head, and said, "Haven't you ever spit on the sidewalk?"

I looked down at my ticket book. I wondered how many cops wore reflective or dark sunglasses like mine, not so much for the glare of the sun, but to hide their shame at having to write petty citations just to keep their stats high enough to please their superiors. I glanced up, but couldn't look the young man directly in the eyes. Instead, I spoke to his deviated septum. "I'm sorry. I don't make the laws. I just enforce them."

And enforce them I did. Week after week, I maintained my spot as one of the top producers on the bicycle squad, but this was the price: upsetting decent people by giving them petty citations. I felt trapped. If I wanted better assignments, or to be looked at for a promotion, I had to produce consistent, impressive numbers.

The man ran his hands through his hair, looked around and muttered, "I can't believe this." His gaze bounced up to me and he spoke a bit louder, angrier. "I'm getting over a cold. I had this, this phlegm, and I just had to get it out or choke on it. I mean, c'mon. Please, sir. There's not even a garbage can nearby."

My right hand twitched with the desire to rip the citation in half, but the words of my sergeant from this morning prevented such a mercy: "Gentleman, if you want to be on a bike, on this squad, we need the numbers." I handed the young man the ticket and, in a flat voice, provided my automatic, memorized explanation of what he needed to do to take care of his citation.

While my lips moved, my mind hauled me back about three years. Stacey and I were in our second year of marriage, living paycheck to paycheck, our first child born only a couple of months before. I sat on the driver's seat of our

2003 Hyundai Elantra. We were merging onto the freeway onramp when a screech erupted behind us and consumed our cab. I clenched my teeth; my body tensed. Our car lurched forward and the Elantra's rear end popped up. Metal groaned. Tires screamed. My seat belt bit a line from left shoulder to right hip. angle, rear bumper mangled. I drew a couple quick, sharp breaths, feeling my heart hammer against my ribs. Remembering I wasn't alone, I reached for my wife with a trembling hand."You okay?"

Stacey was pale. Her lower lip quivered. Tears spilled from her eyes. She gasped, blinked furiously, and twisted to look into the back at our screaming daughter. A man stumbled out of the Altima holding the back of his neck. I exited our car, too. "You okay?" I said to the man. He grimaced at my car, then at something behind me. "You okay?" I asked again. He focused on me and said, "Yeah. Yeah, I think so."

I turned to find a Toyota Tacoma, its front smashed, the bumper hanging askew. The driver, an older man with a beard, more gray than brown, was shaking his head, eyes squeezed shut, lips moving. I ducked into our back seat, stroked Ava's cheek and spoke softly, saying things like, "Daddy's here. It's okay. We're alright. It's alright." I walked around our car, surveying the damage and wondering if it would even be worth it to fix.

Sirens approached and a South Jordan Police car stopped behind the wreck.

A stocky officer with a mustache and dark sunglasses approached each of us, collecting driver's licenses and registrations. We all waited inside our vehicles. Stacey held Ava, rocking and soothing her until her crying ceased and her eyelids grew heavy with sleep. I called our insurance agent while we waited. About ten minutes later, I noticed in my rearview mirror the officer standing beside the Tacoma. He handed the man a ticket. The older man didn't argue, didn't look surprised, just resigned.

The officer approached my open window, bent closer, and offered me my license and registration. I took my paperwork with hands that still shook, though not so badly. "Your license expired yesterday," the officer said, scribbling on a small pad of paper. "Sorry," I said, "I hadn't realized. I'll take care of it first thing tomorrow." The officer handed me a clipboard with a paper attached. He looked at theAltima as he said, "You need to sign here. It's a ticket for your expired driver license."

My hands stopped halfway to the clipboard. I stared at him in disbelief. I swallowed, thinking, *We were just rear-ended, inconvenienced beyond belief by a reckless driver, and now I'm getting a ticket for being expired by one day?* My bewilderment turned to indignation. "Officer," I said, but he interrupted. "Sorry, man, just doing my job." *Sorry, man, just doing my job.*

I had just told this young man who'd spit on the sidewalk nearly verbatim what that South Jordan officer had told me a year before I became a cop. I'd become that officer and this young man had become me. Grimacing, head sinking between my shoulders, I shuffled to my bike and hurried away. My only consolation was in knowing that my supervisor would be satisfied by today's numbers and I wouldn't be the one hauled into his officer for a butt-chewing.

Before becoming a cop, I'd known vaguely, in the back of my mind, that some sort of quota system probably existed, at least to some degree. I just didn't realize how bad it was until now. Later that evening, I met up with one of my best friends on the bike squad. We half sat, half stood on our bicycles, side-by-side on a sidewalk. We watched Pioneer Park and chatted.

"I can't believe I actually gave a guy a ticket for spitting on the sidewalk,"I said. "Aren't we supposed to be peace officers, not so much police officers?" My friend gave me a sideways, quizzical glance. "What do you mean?" I shrugged. "You know, keeping the peace. Making people feel safer. Not micro-managing every behavior, breathing down their necks. I swear, every day more and more people hate us. And why wouldn't they?" My friend chuckled. I shot him a scowl.

"Sorry," he said. "What you're saying isn't funny. I'm just thinking about what our sergeant says he wants next." I winced. "And what's that?" "He's mandating five misdemeanor arrests per day. No matter what. No exceptions." I shook my head. My stomach felt like it was digesting itself. Enough was enough. What were we supposed to do if we didn't witness enough crimes Maybe put a stack of money on a park bench and, when somebody picked it up, tackle the person and arrest them for theft? *A-ha! Gotcha! Five misdemeanor arrests. Sarge will be so proud.*

I wondered if half of the animosity I heard about in the news between people across the country and police was due to this stupid statistical quota system. How easy it must be for a minority to feel picked on, thinking this type of senseless harassment could only be because of his or her race. I could see how trivial things could explode into a more serious situation all over some stats-driven citation. That man who I'd cited for spitting on the sidewalk could've easily gotten loud and aggressive. How would it be trying to explain to internal affairs, or to a jury, how spitting on the sidewalk led to the spitter being tasered or pepper sprayed. Or worse.

"Hey," my friend said, "it's time. Let's go clock out and hope for a better day tomorrow." He snorted loudly, then spit on the grass in front of us. He grinned at me, then pedaled away. I started to smile, but couldn't quite get it to stay. Somebody had to say something. Somebody had to object to this unreasonable push for numbers for the sake of numbers. There had to be a better way to measure success or to motivate officers to do their job. The current way of doing things was turning me into a person I didn't like.

As I followed my friend to the police station, I thought again of the family in the van that we saved from being impounded. I remembered how good that felt to help someone, not crush that guy and his family under the big, black boot of justice in order to get one more number. I wanted to be a cop to help people, to make the world safer, not to harass people over petty infractions. I wanted to be the good guy from the movies, not the bully that everyone loathes to see heading in their direction. But what could I do? How could I complain without getting in trouble? I wanted promotions. I wanted special assignments.I felt trapped in a box. When I finally arrived home and got into bed, it took a long time to fall asleep with all these thoughts in my head.

<hr>

The next day, just as my buddy on the bike squad had said, our sergeant sat us down and gave us his expectation of five misdemeanor arrests per day, per officer. I sat with my hands balled into fists, jaw clenched. I kept telling myself that I had to say something when he was done with his presentation. This whole system of promotion and special assignments and paid time off and other perks based on an officer's stats wasn't right. It wasn't right that our department had to put up certain numbers in order to qualify for federal grant money, or that part of our funding from local sources was rooted in stats, too.

"No." Our sergeant froze mid-sentence. The room plunged into silence, everyone very still. I felt eyes that seemed to drill into my head. I squirmed. My heart felt like a frantic bird trapped at the bottom of my throat, but I'd already spoken aloud.

I was committed. No going back. Our sergeant's eyes narrowed; his lips were a tight, thin line. "What did you say, Moutsos?" "No" I said again. "How can we do this?" I shook my head. "Can you imagine if the citizens of Salt Lake knew we had to arrest five of them each day just to hit a number? What if there's nobody to arrest? What if we get to the end of our shift and only have two? I thought law enforcement was about serving and protecting, not punishing just so we can get an extra day of paid vacation."

Word by word, our sergeant's face grew redder and redder. In a low, hissing voice, he said, "Get out there and do your job. All of you. Go!" We rose and shuffled out, no one speaking, heads bowed, no one making direct eye contact.

At the end of our shift, our squad gathered in the bicycle office for our line down, or debriefing. Most everyone chatted about their day and the calls they had gone on. That's usually how line-down went. Story time of the craziness we went through for the day. Everyone seemed pretty relaxed.

But not me. Our sergeant entered the small room and we sat. He stood behind a table, holding a stack of tickets. He called a name then, one by one, laid down the tickets, counting them off.

"One, two, three, four, five, six. Good." "One, two, three, four, five. Henderson, you barely made it." A few uneasy chuckles puttered through the air. With each name and counting, my heart beat a little faster. The room seemed to shrink and grow hotter. "Moutsos," our sergeant said. "One, two, three..." Our sergeant glared at me. I stared back as calmly as I could. I then blurred my vision to look at him so the intensity and fear didn't overcome me.

His eyes bulged. Lips snarled. Skin reddened. I leaned back in my chair, surprised by the sudden vehemence in that expression. "Moutsos!" Spit flipped off his lips. "Get in the hall. Now!" He spun and stormed outside.

I grimaced and glanced to my right, just enough to notice my best friend on the squad hunch his shoulders and shake his head. I stood. The moment hung across my shoulders like a three-hundred-pound chain. I trudged out of the room. The moment the door closed behind me, our sergeant erupted, jabbing a finger at my face.

"How dare you. You insult me in front of everyone on the squad." A flurry of mother-effers and other curses ensued. "Let me tell you something. You are going to stay after shift and arrest two more people." More cursing, then, "Go tell everyone they're dismissed." Our sergeant whirled and stomped across the parking lot to his unmarked police car. I lifted my chin. Did he really have to talk to me like that? Seriously?I was trying to bring up a legitimate question, not trying to undermine his authority or whatever it was he thought I was doing.

I returned to the bicycle office, glanced at all the expectant faces, and said,"Sarge says you can go home." "Yeah," someone said, "I think we all heard." "Is he really making you stay after to arrest two more people?" one of my partners asked. I nodded. "Looks like it." "I'm with you," another partner said. "This five ticket thing..." Everyone started to leave. I just stared at the piles of five or more tickets on the table. A soft punch to my shoulder seemed to say, *Hang in there, Moutsos, you'll be alright.* Then I was alone.

I waited a moment, then headed outside. As my bicycle squad partners got in their cars and drove home, I heard them call, one by one, to the main radio dispatch that they were 10-42. Off-duty. Not me. I had two arrests to make or I couldn't go home to my wife and kids. Stupid. I yanked open my patrol car door and plopped down on my seat. I huffed and glared sideways at my sergeant, who was still waiting in his car. I pulled out of the underground parking, turned onto the street, then parked at the nearest corner of the nearest intersection. I waited, glaring out my window at the night.

My sergeant parked across the intersection, kitty-corner to me. His sour expression, lit from below by his open laptop, was directed at me. *Fine*, I thought, gritting my teeth. *We'll see how long you want to play this childish game.* He glared at me. I glared at him. Time crawled. I studied the crescent moon. I frowned at traffic. I wriggled on my seat, trying to get more comfortable. I drummed my fingers on the steering wheel.

Stats, like vultures searching for a carcass, circled my thoughts. It seemed to me that writing tickets the way we did was a lot like a fireman starting fires to stay employed, then putting them out to look like the hero. It was a sick game, but I'd have to play that game if I wanted to transfer to a specialty position or promote to sergeant. I barked a humorless laugh.

An hour passed. Our squad walkie talkie crackled. My sergeant said. "Moutsos, go home. We'll talk first thing tomorrow." My sergeant never did speak to me about how I'd complained about his five misdemeanor arrests proposal. A few weeks later, however, one of my partners told me that he'd heard my name brought up in a conversation about stats. Another partner confided a similar experience. I could only hope my reputation wasn't tarnished. Time would tell. Looking back, this seemed to be the turning point of my career with the administration. All because of quotas.

CHAPTER 16

Inspired Question

I coasted on my bike, following the sidewalk around Pioneer Park. The smallish park was notorious for being a hangout of the city's homeless population.Ahead, I spotted a familiar face ambling my way. Robert Jones was a black male in his early forties, a short, thickset guy with an accent that I couldn't quite place, but I suspected Louisiana.

I'd found him passed out drunk too many times to count. Robert noticed me, grinned, and raised a hand in greeting. "What up, Officer Eric?" I slowed to a stop and said, "Robert, what? Where's Bruce? You're always with Bruce." "Oh, he's got some change. Off buying himself a snack. He'll be around soon." His mouth stretched in a toothy grin.

"We can't be the Braveheart Guys without Bruce." "Robert the Bruce," I said, smiling. "You patrolling the park?" Robert said. I hardly heard the question. There was something peculiar about Robert. He almost looked as if... "What's the matter?" Robert said. "Officer Eric?"

My eyebrows shot up in surprise. "Holy cow, Robert, you're stone cold sober." Robert blinked, then wheezed with laughter. "I guess I am." "I don't think I've ever seen you not drunk. You're...You're coherent. We're having a normal conversation.   What's the occasion, Robert?" "I know, man, I know. Things have been rough the last few years. I haven't made the best decisions." "You know," I said, "I've always wondered where you're originally from. You have an accent, but it's always been slurred with booze." Robert puffed up with pride. "Louisiana, sir." I nodded, inwardly pleased that I'd guessed correctly. "So different from Utah," Robert said. "Dry here; wet there."

I opened my mouth to ask more about his home state, but a sudden urgency to know why he'd come to Utah struck me. I paused, confused. It was a natural enough question to ask, but why this sense of need surrounding the question?"Robert," I said, interrupting his explanation of how Louisiana cuisine was superior to that of Utah, "what brought you all the way here from Louisiana?" Robert blinked. The question came to my mind and I knew I had to ask it the way I did. His eyes lost their focus. His smile turned peaceful. "Officer Eric, God told me to come here. I'm still not sure why, but He did. I swear on my life."

An idea popped into my head. A free movie about God played daily at the nearby Legacy Theater, one of the buildings belonging to The Church of Jesus Christ of Latter-Day Saints. I couldn't explain why, but I knew Robert had to see it. I said, "Do you mind if I share a little about what I believe?"

"No, Officer Eric, please do." I spent a while explaining my faith, then told him about the movie. I said, "It plays every hour and a half. Would you like to see it?" Robert chuckled. "I got nothing going on. Sure, I would." I took out my phone and looked up the theater. The next start time was in about fifteen minutes and was the last showing of the day. It would take about twenty minutes to walk there. No good. I had to get Robert there faster. I glanced at his gut and thought, *No way he can run there. Gotta drive.*

My police car was parked about a block away at the nearby substation. I looked at Robert, then toward my car across the street. "Uh, meet me at that corner." I pointed. "Be there in two minutes." I pushed forward and pedaled hard. I reached the substation, secured my bike, jumped in my car, and rushed to the appointed corner. Robert stood there, shaking his head and grinning like this was all a splendid way to pass his evening.

I rolled down the window. "Get in back." Robert obeyed. As I pulled into traffic and headed up the street, a thought jolted me: *I didn't search him before he got in my car. What if he had a weapon? No, Robert is a good enough guy. A drunken nuisance, not violent. But what if he had something illegal on him. No, no, no, just get him to the movie. There's a reason for this. I know it. Stop stressing. But what if...* The entire way there, I argued back and forth with myself.

A few minutes later, I pulled up to South Temple and Main Street. I parked, glanced over my shoulder, and said, "I'll be back after the movie to pick you up right here." Robert nodded and grinned. "Alright, Officer Eric, I'll see you after." I watched him go inside. Was I crazy for doing this? Could I get in trouble with my sergeant if he found out? Despite my misgivings, I knew in my heart that this was what Robert had traveled across the country for. The thought humbled me. I was the one lucky enough to be put in Robert's path.

I ate dinner and patrolled and fortunately, there were no calls or problems that prevented me from being there when Robert sauntered out, the setting sun splashing the city in gold, orange, and pink. Robert got in back, buckled up, and I turned to ask what he thought of the movie, but he spoke first. "Oh, Officer Eric. I loved it. I know that story is true. I could feel God all around me."

I couldn't speak, just smiled faintly, feeling content. I started to drive. Halfway to the shelter, Robert said, "I believe God wants me to go back to my momma's house. I think I'm done with Utah." "Here," I said after we pulled up to the shelter, and handed Robert my card with my cell phone number on the back. "In case you need it." Robert started to get out, but paused. "God bless you, Officer Eric."I nodded, not entirely sure how I should feel about this bizarre day. Robert closed the door, waved, and went inside. "Good luck, Robert," I murmured.

Months later, I received an out-of-state call. I hesitated to answer, as such calls were usually some kind of telemarketing pitch, but something inside told me to respond. "Hello?" I said. "Officer Eric, how you doing?" I barked a surprised laugh. "Robert. Hey, I'm great. Where have you been? I haven't seen you downtown in forever." He chuckled. "I told you, I had to go back to my momma's house." I grinned. Robert sounded great. His voice held real energy and a nuance of purpose. "That's great," I said. "You sound good."

"Better than good," Robert said. "Guess what?" I shrugged. "I give up. What?" "I found your missionaries out here. They came to my momma's house. I'm getting baptized!" Chills tingled my skin. My mouth fell open. I searched for words, but could only say, "That's...that's amazing." "Yep," he said. "It's great. I'm great. Anyway, I was just calling to say thank you. For what you did for me. God is good!"

I shook my head, thinking how I'd almost chickened out of taking him to that movie, how I'd doubted that inner voice when it told me to ask him a specific question --a question that opened the door to this miracle. After this phone call, I promised to never second guess myself again. Robert called about once a month. I looked forward to those calls. They always boosted my spirits and left me with a sense of encouragement. He married a woman he couldn't praise enough. He became a chef in Pennsylvania. Oh, and Momma started going to church, too. The life of a homeless drunk transformed. And all it took was one little, inspired question in my police uniform.

CHAPTER 17

"Not to speak is to speak; not to act is to act."
—UNKNOWN

Moral Police

One weekend in the winter of 2010, my partner and I were patrolling downtown Salt Lake City. A little before midnight, dispatch called for an available officer, or officers, for a medical assist. Several teenagers had overdosed on drugs at a youth dance held weekly at the Salt Palace Convention Center. This was the third weekend in a row where dispatch had made such a call, but my first time responding.

I turned onto West Temple and parked in front of the Salt Palace, a massive, sprawling structure that ran the length of two city blocks. I associated the Salt Palace with international business conventions, national expos for sports or the arts, and Comic-Con. But a youth dance? An ambulance arrived a moment later and parked behind us.

My partner and I greeted the two paramedics and we headed for the entrance, which was below an odd, cylindrical tower of mostly glass, with metal supports which served no apparent purpose. I supposed the architect intended the tower to give the building some structural flair. We entered the first set of glass doors and the umpa-umpa-umpa of muffled techno music thrummed in my ears. Through the second set of doors, in the spacious lobby, the music leapt to a volume that required us to raise our voices, or lean in close to hear one another speak. Just ahead, skittering, pulsing, colorful light surged out of the ballroom's open doors.

A dozen or so teenagers, half of them in only their underwear, stood, squatted, or knelt around two girls lying on the carpeted floor and a boy who sat with his back against the wall and his head hanging between his knees. One of the girls lying on the floor kept twitching, then freezing, twitching then freezing. The boy sitting against the wall pitched sideways. A girl, kneeling beside him, caught the boy and kept him upright. I glanced sideways at my partner. He shrugged nonchalantly, but his eyes were uneasy. We followed the paramedics to the group of teenagers and their overdosing friends.

"Hey," I yelled to my partner, "you good for a minute if I check it out?"He nodded. I headed to the nearest open door, took two steps inside, and froze. My eyes widened; my mouth hung open. Thousands of people twitched in chaotic rhythm, flailing arms, jumping in place, pumping fists. Hundreds twirled glow sticks. This was, by far, the largest dance I'd ever seen. Despite the cavernous size of the ballroom, it was packed. On one side, there were a couple of inflatable bounce houses--actual freaking bounce houses.

Movement to my right snagged my attention. In the shadows, a pale, scrawny girl in her bra and panties, age fourteen or fifteen at most, clung to an older boy who shoved his tongue in her mouth while vigorously massaging her butt with both hands. I recoiled and took a step backwards. I tripped, threw my hands out, and caught my balance. I looked down and glared at what I'd nearly fallen over. Snow boots. Then I noticed what was piled along the wall as far as I could see: coats, hats, gloves, boots, pants, and shirts. Well, that explained why all the kids were half naked.

I noticed something else and my stomach dropped and clenched. Teenagers with baby pacifiers; others with medical masks that covered their mouth and nose. People who took ecstasy often clamped and ground their jaw so hard they chipped a tooth. The pacifiers prevented the side-effect by giving them something soft to chew on. Plus, due to the purported, heightened physical senses that ecstasy created, it felt good to have something in one's mouth. The masks would be lined with vapor rub, used to intensify the drug's high.

Everywhere, teenagers, and many too old to be teenagers, rubbed up on each other, grinding and making out. I glanced at the bounce houses and could only imagine what happened inside. *This isn't a youth dance,* I thought. *This is a full-on rave.* I struggled to wrap my mind around what was happening. Raves were usually held in abandoned warehouses, not in the largest convention center in Salt Lake City. This was advertised as a weekly youth dance. Mommy and daddy were naively dropping their kids off at a massive rave.

And there, like an island in the middle of a turbulent sea, stood the security detail for the evening: thirteen off-duty Salt Lake City Police Officers. They laughed amongst themselves, pointing now and then at something they found especially hilarious. I thought: *We're supposed to break up raves like this, not chaperone them.*

Was I making this into a bigger deal than it was? I mean, there were off-duty cops keeping things under control. Maybe this wasn't so bad. These kids would do this anyway, so why not make it a safer environment, right? Right? I shook my head. I tried to justify what I was seeing, but each argument in favor of this situation smacked into a wall of truth. This reminded me of those parents you sometimes heard about, the ones who threw parties with alcohol for their kids and their friends so they could supervise. When arrested, they always said the same thing: "Our kids would do it anyway, so I wanted to make sure they did it in a safe environment."

I wondered if our department's administration knew what was going on here. Someone grabbed my arm. I flinched, whirled, and put a hand to my gun. My partner arched an eyebrow. "Relax, Moutsos," he shouted. "Come on.""We left the ballroom. I said, "How many people do you think come to these dances?" He shrugged. "I heard anywhere from five to seven thousand." I nodded towards the paramedics and the overdosed teenagers. "Are they okay?" "They'll be fine." He handed me a sheet of notebook paper. "Here." I frowned at the names and phone numbers.

"Those are the kids and those are their parents' phone numbers. Will you start calling, while I see if the paramedics need anything else?" I nodded and began the awkward calls to parents. Hi, Mr. or Mrs. So-And-So, your kid overdosed. Come and take them home. Oh, and by the way, that seemingly innocent youth dance you dropped them off at was actually a drug-fueled orgy. Thank you. You have a nice day, too. I sighed, retrieved my cell phone, and dialed the first number.

The next Saturday night, my partner for that shift and I responded to another overdose at the Salt Palace Convention Center. The overdosing girl was mostly incoherent. She'd appear lucid every few minutes, so I'd ask a question, but before she could answer, her eyes would roll up in her head and she'd babble. She vomited twice. Her friends weren't much help. They claimed that they didn't know what was wrong with her. Drugs? No, we don't do drugs. She's proba-

bly just sick, they'd say, and look everywhere but at my
face.

The paramedics wheeled the girl out on a gurney and
loaded her into the back of their ambulance, where they
gave her fluids intravenously. A few minutes after reaching
the ambulance, the girl's mother arrived on scene. Wild-
eyed, she cried out, "My baby. Where's my baby?" My partner waved her over. Mom rushed to the back of the ambulance. She gawked at her daughter, then at me, back and
forth several times. Finally, Mom jabbed a finger in her
daughter's direction and said, "Why is my thirteen-year-old
daughter in her bra and underwear?"

Her words felt like a punch to my gut. I wanted to shrink
inside my coat like a turtle retreating inside its shell. Of
course, I knew the reason, but I just shrugged.
 The girl's mom turned her frantic attention on the paramedics. "Don't you have a blanket or something? It's freezing." The two paramedics blinked at one another, then one
of them retrieved a blanket. My partner gave Mom a hand
up and inside the back of the ambulance where she fussed
over her worn-out daughter. I faced the Salt Palace and
glared, my hands balled so tightly into fists that they shook.

Later that night, at the end of my shift, I strode into my
sergeant's small office, shutting the door behind me. Without preamble, I said, "Do you not see what's going on?" My
sergeant rolled his eyes. "What's going on with what?" "The

Salt Palace," I said. He frowned and cocked his head to the side. "You're talking about the overdoses?" "The dance is a freaking rave." My sergeant cocked an eyebrow, an expression that said, "You're being a little melodramatic, aren't you?" "The kids, the drugs, the overdoses," I said. "The police working the event. Do you not see how this is a problem?"

"Moutsos, you need to relax. What are you the moral police?" He spoke calmly, but I could tell he was bothered. "Sir, I don't think you understand. These parents are dropping their kids off at what they think is a youth dance. They see the police cars parked there, so they think it's safe, good, clean fun." My sergeant opened his mouth, but I rushed on in a voice made tighter and tighter by anger. "Inside, those kids are getting drugs, overdosing, and probably being sexually assaulted by some pervert in any number of dark corners. The girl who overdosed tonight was thirteen. I saw men inside that dance who had to be in their late twenties, if not thirties. And our guys are there, playing security, with all this happening around them."

My sergeant sighed. "All right. All right. What do you want me to do?" "It needs to stop. Now. If you don't do something about it, I will." "I'll make a call; see what I can do." I nodded, thanked my sergeant, and headed home. After a few days off and before I headed out on my next patrol shift, my sergeant called me to his office. I entered and found him sitting behind his desk. "Hey, Moutsos, I wanted to let you know that I talked with the lieutenant about what you told me." I nodded and waited for him to go on.

"Anyway, everything is good now." "What do you mean, good?" I said. He shrugged. "Well, there's nothing wrong with our department working at the dance. We do security for a lot of events. And the lieutenant and I agree, it's better we're there to watch over things." I snarled, yanked my gloves on, and stormed out. My sergeant's voice chased me. "Moutsos, you're making this a bigger deal than it is." I growled, muttered and shook my head. I felt bad for the officer who was assigned to be my partner for this shift. In my mood, I wouldn't be the most pleasant to work with.

The following Sunday, Stacey and I took our kids to my parents' house for dinner. My older sister, younger brother, and younger sister were also there. While everyone enjoyed their meal and each other's company, I hunched over the table and, with my fork, shoved what was left of my roast around my plate, circle after circle, until my food was one big mashed potato-covered mess.

"Eric. Eric!" I lifted my head and blinked at those around me. I'd been so inwardly focused that I wasn't sure who called my name. My mom said, "Eric, what's wrong?" I grimaced at my plate of uneaten food. "Nothing." Silence. I looked back up. Mom arched an eyebrow and waited. Only the kids were still eating. Everyone else waited for me to speak. I rolled my eyes and huffed. "Son," my dad said, "what's going on?"

I looked to Stacey, as if she'd have some magical way out for me. She shrugged, her expression saying, *Tell them, Eric. They're your parents.* I started out mumbling vaguely about the "youth dances" at the convention center. However, the more I talked, the more irritated I became, and the more forcefully the details poured out. Mom stared at me with wide eyes and a hand over her mouth. Dad sat very still and tight-lipped, which meant that inside, he was truly upset. "I can't believe someone higher up hasn't reprimanded those officers," Mom said.

"I complained to my sergeant," I said. Dad slapped the tabletop. "And what did he do?" I snorted. "He talked to the lieutenant." "And the lieutenant...?" Dad gestured for me to continue. "He told my sergeant, and my sergeant told me, that it was all just fine and dandy. Better for officers to be there to watch over the kids. Make sure nothing really, really bad happens. It seems I'm making this into a bigger deal than it actually is." "Well," Mom said, "that sergeant and lieutenant must not know how bad it is."

I shrugged. "They might not have seen what goes on there in person, but they have the reports. They know there are weekly overdoses by kids as young as thirteen." "If they won't do something," Mom said, "then somebody else needs to, before some parents' little boy or girl dies." My brother said, "I could call Salt Lake City PD and make an anonymous complaint. Maybe that would do something." My sisters wanted to do the same, both of them talking over each other, brainstorming aloud. I winced and clenched my teeth. *Yeah,* I thought. *Somebody does need to do something, but anonymous complaints might not be enough.*

―――※◈※―――

Next Saturday was the coldest day of the year. Clear night skies had made for ridiculously frigid temperatures. Christmas waited right around the corner. I stood outside our substation across from Pioneer Park, chatting with one of my partners--it was uncomfortably hot inside, so he'd wanted some fresh air."No way," my partner said, "it's going to be the Patriots and Packers in the Super Bowl. Aaron Rodgers is on fire. Did you see the..." Movement on the sidewalk behind my partner grabbed my attention."Hey," I said, "that's a kid." "What?" my partner said, and turned. He cursed under his breath.

A boy, around fourteen years old, stumbled along the sidewalk, heading our way. He wore only a white t-shirt and what I initially believed to be shorts, but realized were only boxers. *Kid in his underpants,* I thought, blinking, wondering if this was real or an apparition. About ten yards away, the wobbly teenager dropped to his knees. He made a pitiful noise, like a wounded animal. My partner and I rushed to either side of him."Hey," I said, and gave him a shake. "You okay?" my partner said.

The teenager's head flopped back. He mumbled a few incoherent words."He's high on something," my partner said. "Look at his eyes." I stood and called dispatch on my radio, requesting immediate medical assistance. "Hey," my partner said. "He's an ice cube. Let's get him inside." We carried the boy inside, sat him on a chair, found a blanket, and wrapped it around him. The boy shivered and his teeth chattered behind blue lips."Why were you outside?" I said. "Why are you dressed like this?" "The dance," the boy said in a slurred, petulant tone. "She was so nice. She shared it with me, shared it all, then it was gone. Poof-poof." Comprehension slammed into place. My eyes narrowed and my voice came out rougher than I intended. "What dance?"

The boy's brown, dilated eyes rolled my way. "The salty one." He giggled."The Salt Palace," I said. "You mean that dance?" "Uh-huh," the boy said. "You took something," I said. "The girl gave you drugs?" The boy groaned. "Don't call my dad. I won't do it again." "Why'd you walk all the way here on a night like tonight?" my partner said."Not that far," the boy said. His shivering subsided. He looked pale and started to perspire.

Worried that the boy might vomit, I snatched a nearby garbage can, but he just slouched on his chair and looked sleepy. "That stupid dance." I stood, fists trembling at my sides. At no time in my career to this point had I felt more indignation than I did at that moment. We, the cops, were sanctioning this. I ground my teeth so hard I thought they'd crack. I wanted to punch something, take that garbage can and hurl it against a wall.

I heard the ambulance and stormed up the walkway to greet the paramedics. The next morning, just after I woke up, I found the phone number to our chief of police. May as well go right to the top. Besides, he claimed to have an open-door policy. I texted him: "This is Officer Moutsos and it's really important that I speak with you. Very sorry to bother you on a Sunday."

I ate breakfast with my family, showered, then helped Stacey get the kids ready for church. The chapel was so close that, despite the cold, we walked. Halfway there, my cell phone rang and vibrated. I flinched and my heart jumped then pounded. I checked the number. The chief, calling me back.

My two oldest children decided, at that moment, to start arguing. To Stacey, I said, "I gotta take this." I whirled and ran back the other way, leaving my poor wife to break up a fight and get the kids to church. I took a deep breath and answered the call. "Good afternoon, Officer Moutsos," the chief said. "I got your text. How may I help you?" "There's, um, a problem, sir. I've tried my chain of command and it went nowhere. Somebody has to know--somebody has to let you know."

Chief Cainam was silent a moment then said, "Go on." The whole story gushed out of me. When I finished, I sagged against the wall just inside my house, the phone seeming to weigh fifty pounds. "That's about it, sir," I said. Silence. I had just begun to suspect a dropped call when the chief finally spoke."Unbelievable. Thank you, Officer Moutsos. I will look into this personally and do what needs to be done." I took a few minutes to compose myself and collect my thoughts, then headed back to church.

Soon I learned what happened to the youth dance at the Salt Palace. I was sitting at my dining room table, munching on a sandwich and grapes and checking the local news on my phone. The headline "Weekend Rave Lands Several in Jail." I clicked on the link and read the article, my lunch forgotten. I dropped my phone on the table and shoved my chair back. I shook my head. Seriously? The article was all about how the police swooped in and saved the children. All positive. Nothing about cops being paid to do security by the people putting on the corrupt dance. Nothing about how security watched it all happen, week after week and never did anything. No one held accountable. Cainam played it perfectly. Another article came out, "Party Organizers Defend So-Called Rave."

One of the articles read: "Salt Palace General Manager Allison Jackson says they don't discriminate against any event, even during the Christmas season when families are walking around downtown. "All types of people have the right to celebrate how they want to celebrate," she said. Jackson apologized if some families saw some scantily dressed people as they were passing through the Salt Palace. But she said, "I can't control how people dress. Jackson said Salt Lake police like it when dances like the "Naughty and Nice Rave" is held at the Salt Palace because it is a controlled environment. "They would much rather have it with us than in a warehouse or underground where they are not sure what is happening." She said she was not aware of the drug arrests during the party."

Well, I thought, *at least the raves were stopped.* A few days later, I sat in my patrol car and my phone rang. "Hello. This is Officer Moutsos." "Moutsos," a man said, his voice turning my last name into something repulsive. "Who the hell do you think you are?" "Excuse me," I said, sitting taller and scowling. "Who is this?""Lieutenant Black."

I flinched. Why in the world was he calling me? He wasn't my lieutenant."You the moral police now? Huh?" I gave my head a shake and tried to make sense of this bizarre call. "We all had a hell of a gig going until you ruined it. Five thousand for each night, that's what you cost us." "Cost you for what?" "You are stupid, aren't you?" Something clicked inside my head. I blinked, incredulous. "Is this about the raves at the Salt Palace?"

"Yeah," he said. "You got a lot of people pissed. You cost us $5,000 per night," he said again. "You..." I waited, my mouth hanging open. The lieutenant cleared his throat, then said, "Who do you think you are, Moutsos? Have a nice day, friend."

I started to reply, but he hung up. I grimaced at my phone. Did that really just happen? I stared out my windshield at the darkening sky. *Whatever,* I thought. *It's over and done.* But it wasn't. Not really. Gossip and the rumor mill were as unforgiving as a lieutenant who believed himself cheated out of a lucrative security deal. I was now a tattletale. I was now the "moral police." And some police don't like being policed. Especially, and ironically, the very lieutenant who stopped the complaint I made weeks earlier.

CHAPTER 18

"The first step in getting better at not pre-judging is to stop pre-judging."
—SETH GODIN

Pre Judging

My shoulders sagged a bit as I entered the Pioneer Patrol Building on the west side of the city. My time with the bike squad was over. I was pushed out a rotation early. The experience had been awesome, the best part of my career as far as camaraderie went, but it had to end sometime. Now I was back to patrol.

I liked patrol, I told myself, and nodded. This isn't a bad thing, just a temporary thing. A normal stepping stone in my career. The voice of my police academy sergeant interrupted my thoughts. "You want to be stuck in patrol your whole career? You sorry bunch of losers. Shapeup or that'll be where you end up. Forever. You'll never go anywhere but patrol if you keep screwing around!"

Patrol: the trenches of police work; land of new officers; the preferred assignment for those who wanted to do real police work; the limbo between specialty positions; the career graveyard for those blacklisted by upper administration. I wondered if I was on that administrative blacklist. I'd certainly ruffled some tail feathers. *No,* I thought as I straightened, lifting my chin. *Attitude is the small thing that makes the big difference.*

I pulled a pen from my shirt pocket and studied the openings available to me, laid out in simple papers lists on a table where each Sergeant had left them for sign-ups.   There weren't many choices. I found the shift I needed, placed the tip of my pen to an open slot, and froze. Sergeant Winn.

I hung my head and squeezed my eyes shut, thinking, *Oh, no. Not him.* I'd never worked for Winn, but I'd heard plenty of rumors. If I wanted the shift with the schedule that best fit my needs, then this was the only option. I signed my name and headed home.

When I arrived home that night, I found my wife writhing on the couch, teeth gritted, eyes squeezed shut, and tears rolling down her cheeks. My heart leapt; terror wound my muscles tight. I rushed to her. Had there been an accident with one of our kids? We had two girls and a boy and Stacey was pregnant with our fourth, another girl. "Babe," I said, and took a knee beside her, "what's the matter?" Stacey opened her eyes. Her lips twisted. A sob escaped. *Please, I*

thought, *let the baby be okay*. I ran a hand through her hair
and searched for something comforting to say.

"I don't know what's wrong," she finally said, sniffling.
"It's my back. The pain comes and goes." "Should I take
you to the hospital?" Stacey winced, thought it over, then
shook her head. "Not yet. I think it's getting better." "Is it...I
don't know, like a really bad pregnancy cramp?" She shook
her head. "This is different. I don't know what it is."
"Maybe you threw your back out?" I said. "Pulled a muscle?
Pinched nerve?" Stacey shrugged. "Could be." I kissed her
forehead, which left a sweat-salty taste on my lips.

"Go change out of your uniform," Stacey said. "I'll be
okay. The pain is already fading." I nodded, rose, and rushed
to our bedroom to change. An hour later, Stacey was feeling
much better, so we sat at the kitchen table for a late dinner
of leftovers, the kids having fallen asleep before I arrived
home. Around a mouthful of chicken, I said, "You'll never
guess who my only choice for sergeant was." "No, I won't
guess. So tell me. Who?""Sgt. Winn." "You don't sound
happy about it." I spread butter across half a roll. "I've never
heard anything good about him." "But you've never personally had him as a supervisor, right?"

"No," I said, "but someone whose judgment I trust told me
that Winn is the type of guy who probably became a cop because he was bullied as a kid and is now power hungry, a
big chip on his shoulder. Every time I hear Winn mentioned,

it's negative." Stacey frowned thoughtfully, then said, "Well, you should give him a chance." I swallowed a bite of roll and gestured with the remaining piece. "You don't understand, everybody says the same thing. No personality. A micro-manager. You cross him and he'll destroy you." Stacey lowered her fork, leaned closer, and said, "Eric, aren't there some people in the department that don't like you so much?" I stiffened and grimaced. "Like the cops who worked the rave at the Salt Palace--and that lieutenant, too?" "Yeah," I said, "but--"

"And your last sergeant, the one who demanded a minimum number of misdemeanor arrests. Do you think he talks nicely about you behind your back?" I huffed. "Stacey--" "No," she said, "what they probably say about you isn't true. So maybe what some people say about this new sergeant of yours is also not true." "Okay, okay," I said. "I'll give him a chance." Stacey nodded, smirked, and harpooned some green beans with her fork.

As I continued eating in silence, I thought, *If she's wrong, it's going to be a long three months before I can transfer out of there.*

On my first day back on patrol, I skulked into the break room for my first fifteen-minute lineup briefing with Sgt. Winn. My gaze swept the other unfortunate souls who'd signed up for this shift. I noticed two familiar faces, a couple of guys from the academy, and a bit of the tension released from between my shoulders. I nodded at one of them.

The officer returned my nod and gave me a small, welcoming smile. *Okay,* I thought, *I might at least have a good crew to work with.* Not wanting to draw Sgt. Winn's attention, I chose a seat near the back of the room. I remained quiet despite lineup usually being a time to chat and joke around when not discussing police business and what was happening around the city. A moment after I sat, Sgt. Winn entered and commenced with a perfunctory roll-call. Everyone was present.

"The only thing I expect is that you handle your calls and watch each other's backs," Sgt. Winn said, his steady gaze cutting a line from one side of the room to the other. "Your number one priority is to get back to your families." *Hmm, I* thought, *yeah, I'm sure that's all you expect.* I grimaced, wondering how I'd become so jaded so quickly. It happened to everyone in law enforcement to some degree or another. I just didn't like it surfacing in me. Still, I couldn't help but suspect Sgt. Winn of being one of those guys who promoted and drank the proverbial Kool-aid, a puppet of upper administration. However, Winn was in patrol and anyone stuck in patrol was usually there because they were the opposite of a puppet. They bucked the system, then paid the price.

That night, I went out and had a blast. I wondered why I ever left patrol. We went on hot calls, raced around the city...It was fantastic. Near the end of my shift, when I had a moment, I called Stacey to tell her about the first day back on patrol. She didn't answer, which wasn't like her, but I didn't let it worry me. I'd just tell her all about it when she called back.

My next call from dispatch dealt with a runaway juvenile. I hadn't dealt with a case like that in at least three years, so I refreshed my memory by looking up our policy, but the specifics of the case were such that policy didn't help resolve the issue. I spoke to a couple officers on our squad, but their only advice was to run it by Sgt. Winn. I groaned and thought, *No way.* I had to make a quick decision and did what I thought was right given the circumstances. I wrote my report, reviewed it, then sent it to Sgt. Winn for approval.

Within the next hour, I noticed a message on my computer from Sgt. Winn that said: I need to talk to you. Meet me at the station. I closed my eyes, sank back against my car seat, and took a deep breath. I wondered what I'd done, or hadn't done. I drove to the station. The closer I came, the stronger my sense of dread. I parked, took a few deep breaths, and went in to Sgt. Winn's office. He stared at me, an interested but otherwise unreadable expression on his tight face.

Uncomfortable, I said, "Sergeant, you wanted to see me."
"Ya, I read your report and wanted to know why you did
what you did?" I shrugged, shifted my feet, and explained
my reasoning. I finished and Winn said, "Good job." I
blinked. He said, "It was a complicated situation, but that
was the right thing to do. I just wanted to tell you that in
person." He smiled. I opened my mouth, but his smile
kicked all thoughts out of my head. I had never seen him
smile before, not even the few times that, over the years, I'd
seen him in passing at the station, or training, or some other
police-related event.

Finally, I nodded. I might've muttered, "Thank you," or
might have only thought that I did. Either way, I walked out
of his office happy, but confused. My shift ended and I went
home. The house was silent and dim, everyone asleep. In
our bedroom, I removed my gear and changed from uniform
to shorts and t-shirt. On my way to the bathroom to brush
my teeth, I stopped by Stacey's side of the bed, stooped and
kissed her forehead. Her skin felt too warm. Frowning, I
pressed my palm to her brow. Definitely running a fever. I
shook her shoulder. Stacey moaned, but didn't wake. I shook
harder.

She muttered, but didn't open her eyes. I rushed to the
medicine cabinet, snatched the infrared forehead thermome-
ter, and returned. 103 degrees. I double-checked. Still 103. I
grabbed my phone and called Stacey's mom, who lived

about twenty minutes away. "Bobbie, it's Eric. Sorry about calling so late." "Eric, what?"

"Can you come over? I think I need to take Stacey to the hospital.""What's wrong?" "I'm not sure. She's having trouble waking up." "Eric--" "She's got a fever. Can you watch the kids?" "Yes. Yes. I'll be right over."

I hung up. I turned towards the bathroom, then towards the bedroom door, then back to Stacey. I ran my hand through my hair and exhaled, trying to think.She was breathing, but lethargic and feverish. She wasn't feeling well yesterday, that pain in her back. A muscle relaxer and some prescription painkillers? Did we even have any of that lying around the house? There's no way should could have taken anything like that while she was pregnant, right? Had she gone to the doctor? She would've called me if she'd gone to the doctor's office.

I glared at the clock. *Come on, Grandma,* I thought. *Hurry.* I shook Stacey and said, "Babe. Babe, come on. Wake up." She groaned and her eyes rolled behind their lids. I shook her harder. I patted her cheek. "Honey. Stacey." "Wha...?" Her eyelids fluttered. "Eric?" "Yeah, babe. It's me. Hey, your mom's coming over." "My mom?" "I'm taking you to the hospital." Her face twisted in pain. "It hurts." "What hurts?" Stacey moaned. "Your back?" I said. She whimpered, closed her eyes tight, nodded, and curled into a ball.

I grabbed shoes for me, slippers for Stacey. I snatched a water bottle for each of us. I peeked out the window at the street. Headlights. Maybe Stacey's mom? I rushed to the bedroom, grabbed Stacey beneath her arms, and hoisted.She leaned heavily against me. I supported most of her weight and muttered a prayer as I helped my wife to the car. The garage door opened and Stacey's mom stopped, stared at us for a beat, then rushed forward. "Eric, what is it?"

I explained the situation in a breathless rush as I helped Stacey into the car. My hands shook so badly that I had to try three times before I could buckle her seat belt. Halfway to the hospital, I thought, *Crap, I hope Grandma closed the garage door.* I glanced sideways at Stacey, who moaned, teeth gritted, eyes squeezed shut. *Who cares about the garage door? Why am I even thinking about the garage door?*

We arrived at the hospital, luckily not hitting every red light along the way.I rushed around the car and pulled Stacey out. The emergency room seemed like a dream; everything in my peripheral was a blur, everything except Stacey going unnoticed. Questions about insurance. Blood pressure check. Temperature check. Questions. Automatic answers. I felt much like a passenger in the back of my own head. Stacey went limp and almost fell. I caught her. Her head lolled against my arm. "Babe." I patted her cheek. "Babe?" Stacey groaned. Nurses surrounded us and helped me get Stacey to her feet.

Her eyes fluttered open. She looked at me and said, "How long have we been here?" Stacey in a hospital gown, in a hospital bed, wheeled away for testing by hospital employees. Waiting. I jerked awake. I straightened, blinked, and looked around at the waiting room. I rubbed my face. I felt like dough, beaten, kneaded, smashed, and stretched flat by a rolling pin. "Mr. Moutsos." I squinted at the woman in scrubs, a stethoscope around her neck. "Yeah, yeah, sorry. What?"

"The scan showed kidney stones blocking both ureters, with twenty-two more stones floating around. Nothing has been passing out of the kidneys and she now has double kidney infections. We need to do a surgery." I nodded, mouth open. "Okay," I said. "Surgery won't be for a while. In the meantime, we're working on the infection and getting her fever down." "Surgery," I said.

"Routine," the doctor, or nurse, or whoever this was said. "Outpatient surgery. She's doing okay. If you want to follow me, I'll take you to her room." I nodded and followed, feeling a bit more optimistic. The kidney blockage sounded bad, but at least they knew what was wrong and what to do. Stacey slept, hooked up to an IV and monitors. I slouched on the padded chair beside her bed, stuffed a pillow behind my head, and dozed off and on as hospital staff entering every now and then.Uncomfortable hours passed. Stacey mostly slept. When awake, I held her hand and tried to be reassuring, sometimes rubbing her shoulders or feet. Later that morning, Stacey phoned her mom.

The kids were in good hands. I left a message with my sergeant, dreading what he'd say about me not coming in for a few days. I hoped my message was at least coherent and not the ramblings of a sleep-deprived, worry-sick husband. Eventually, they wheeled my wife and her hospital bed away for surgery. I couldn't sleep, so I mostly paced, sometimes playing on my phone and sending a few messages to family, notifying them of what had happened. Our nurse, a lumpy, motherly woman in her later years, knocked and peeked in the room.

I perked up. "Mr. Moutsos, your wife is okay, but there's been a complication with the baby. The anesthesia has worn off of your wife, but the baby isn't waking up. We've started the process of admitting Stacey to the hospital and--" "Our baby," I said, standing up. "Yes, Mr. Moutsos. Nothing to panic about. We're just concerned and want that baby awake and kicking before we discharge your wife."

"Can I see her?" "We'll bring her back here in a bit. I'm not sure when, but not long. I'm sorry. Can I get you anything?" I shook my head and plopped down onto the edge of the chair, slumping, feeling dizzy with fatigue and shock. I prayed and prayed. I didn't know what else I could do. About an hour later, Stacey rolled into the room on her hospital bed. I sprang to my feet, adrenaline cutting back some of the mental fog."Stacey?"

My wife was pale, drowsy, and seemed inexplicably smaller than I remembered her being. Maybe it was all the blankets piled over her.Stacey opened her droopy eyelids; her lethargic gaze found me."The baby?" I said. "You and the baby?" "We're okay," she said in a raspy voice. I exhaled and my shoulders slumped. "Thank goodness." Some mentally muddled hours later, near sunset, we left the hospital, bottles of medications in hand.

My mom came over and Stacey's mom went home. When I was finally able to lay down and crash, I slept for nine hours straight. The next day, I left Stacey and the kids with her parents and headed to work.

I rehearsed different things to say and what I'd say if Sgt. Winn said this or that. My stomach twirled queasily. What if he refused my requests to take certain days off? My parents and Stacey's parents couldn't be there every night I worked and Stacey was on bed rest, unable to help the kids, let alone help herself. She had stints in her ureters. I had to remember to tell Sgt. Winn there were stints and bedrest. That sounded urgent, a compelling reason to be home when I needed to be. I fidgeted through roll call, hardly hearing what was said. When everyone on the squad had left, I remained behind to face Sgt. Winn."Uh, sir, can I speak with you for a moment?" Sgt. Winn nodded. I cleared my throat and said,

"Well, uh..." He waited, arms folded, studying my face. In a rush, I explained what was happening. He listened patiently, calmly, never interrupting. "And," I said, "I guess that's about it."

Sgt. Winn waited a moment, then shook his head. "Moutsos, why don't you go home." "Sir?" "Family first. Be there for your wife. Make your kids feel they're safe." I blinked, nodded, and said, "Okay." I shuffled out, feeling disoriented. All the scenarios in my head and this hadn't been among them. I was able to take time off, even with our squad being short-staffed. I got into my car, grinned, and drove home.

The next three months proved to be the hardest of our lives up to that point. Stacey could barely function as a mom and couldn't even ride in a car because the bumps in the road caused her so much pain. It took a toll on all of us, emotionally and physically. But we did what we had to do until the baby arrived. She and Stacey were both fine in the end, but it was rough going for those months of bed rest.

Sgt. Winn proved to be one of the best supervisors and one of the best people I'd had the honor of knowing. How all those rumors about him began and were perpetuated I'd never know, but I learned a valuable lesson about prejudging someone based on rumors and hearsay.

CHAPTER 19

"The only thing worse than not having a job is having a bad boss."
—UNKNOWN

Motor School

I sat in my patrol car watching traffic. My cell phone rang. "Hello," I said. "Who do you think you are, telling me what you're going to do?" I flinched. I frowned at my phone, then put it back to my ear and said, "I'm sorry. Who--?" "Who do you think, Moutsos?" "Sarge?" I said. I had recently been assigned to this new sergeant, an egomaniac with a badge. Bad combination. Definitely not Sgt Winn. "That's right. Your sergeant. The guy who tells you what to do, not the other way around." "Sir, I don't understand. What--?"

"Your quarterly training voicemail," he barked. "You don't tell me you have a physical fitness exam, and that you're coming onto your shift late. You ask me first, and I okay it, or I don't. Understood?" "Yes, sir. I didn't mean to disrespect. It won't happen again." Silence. He'd disconnected.

I shook my head, thinking how I'd been cordial, even friendly, with this guy for years before he became my supervisor. Why was he acting like this? Three other officers from his shift were with me at the training and they hadn't even called to let him know, just put themselves on the schedule and assumed all was good. At least I'd given him the courtesy of a heads-up, which wasn't really necessary. Sergeants always checked the schedule. He should already know what I was doing.

I sunk back against my seat and closed my eyes. Why was he treating me this way? And it wasn't just this phone call. More than any other supervisor, he'd nitpicked my reports, always sending them back to fix something absurdly insignificant. I'd even caught him parked around a corner, watching me--spying on me. I'd see on the computer, on many occasions, his car parked nearby on the GPS while I was responding to a call. I'd talked to several officers on the squad who I trusted and they'd never heard of him doing anything like that before. Was I a suspect or a cop?

Bike squad was the only thing I could think of. His attitude must stem from the rumors about me being insubordinate, not wanting to play the quota game. My sergeant must've bought into the worst of those rumors, which I'd tried to ignore. I figured they'd go away if I worked hard enough. Didn't my numbers prove I worked hard? I was always at or near the top while on bike squad despite my misgivings about quotas as a means to pressure officers to perform.

I sighed, rubbed my face, and took a deep breath. I exhaled slowly. I reached over to my laptop and checked my emails. My eyes widened. Motorcycle Squad was accepting new applicants. Four spots open. I'd always fantasized about the motorcycle squad, though to be honest, they did terrify me a bit. But my current sergeant terrified me more.

I clicked on the link and started filling out my application. My finger hovered over the keyboard. I hesitated. Did I really want motors? Motor school was notorious for injuries. Broken bones, usually legs. Was it worth the risk of medical bills to get away from my current sergeant? I sent the resume.

Weeks later I stood with the other finalists, watching in awe as the veteran motor cops weaved through a series of complicated maneuvers. Amazing. So fluid. They made it appear easy. After a week of motorcycle school, I felt like I could hardly get out of first gear without killing the engine. What had I expected? I'd never ridden a street bike before. And yet, somehow, I managed to pass each obstacle and move on to the next. I didn't know which was the greater miracle: that I passed to the next round, or that I was still alive.

The week-long school had sent three officers to the hospital. Thirteen had applied. There were four slots open. All we had to do was pass the next day of testing and the job was ours. I offered a silent prayer. I knew God was there. I'd experienced His help throughout my career too often to deny the existence of a higher power. I had faith that if this was the right direction for my life, then my plea for help would be answered. The veteran motor cops sped away, leaving just the motor school's trainers behind with the rest of us.

The motorcycle training sergeant yelled to be heard over the departing roar of engines. "All right, get on your bikes and start driving the intersection. You know the drill." We donned our helmets; the engines thrummed and growled. We headed, single file, to the "intersection," a training course that, if seen from above, looked like a giant plus sign, simulating a typical intersection of a city street. We began the maneuvers, making a sharp turn, left or right, around orange cones placed at the end of each section.

We came around, back into position, and went again. I'd driven this course enough to feel competent and at ease. Then I noticed the trainers and the sergeant approaching. One trainer held two two-by-fours in one hand and a hammer in the other. A second trainer wielded a thick chain and a six-foot iron rod. A third trainer carried a large water gun. The sergeant carried...a used diaper? I grimaced. My hands tightened on the handlebars.

Trainers tossed their items onto the intersection in random places. The course just got a lot more challenging. "Don't you dare stop!" yelled the sergeant. "Run them over!" I clenched my jaw; my body tensed. Thud-thunk, thud-thunk. I bounced over the two-by-fours and hammer. I remained upright. Sweat beaded along my forehead just below the edge of my helmet.

I turned and ran over a pair of shoes. I turned again. Water sprayed the side of my helmet. I flinched. The front wheel jerked and I almost lost it. Around and around we went. From the corner of my eye, I saw the diaper hurtling through the air. "Keep going," the training sergeant yelled. "Don't you dare stop!" On and on the test went. I didn't know how long we'd been at it, but it seemed nearly an hour. I was getting tired, but I was also getting better, fine- tuning the clutch and throttle. I managed a grim smile. I started to enjoy the obstacles. Their added adversity forced me to improve. "Stop!" the sergeant shouted. I halted.

"Your next test is timed." The sergeant pointed at a strip of blacktop dotted with orange cones. "You weave through the cone patterns. Go too slow and you're finished. Got it?" "Yes, sir!" we shouted, nearly in unison, and lined up as ordered. My turn came. I filled my lungs and exhaled a gust of air. I charged. I weaved. I snaked, juked, and jived. My bike now felt a part of me. I felt good, better than I had ever felt on the bike, despite the challenging course.

I can do this, I thought. *I can--* The world jerked sideways. I skidded. A thousand pounds of motorcycle pinned my left foot to the ground, under the foot guard. Someone was screaming. *I* was screaming. Two training officers rushed to me. They heaved the bike upright."Moutsos?" the sergeant yelled. "How bad?" The two training officers exchanged a worried look. One of the trainers muttered for my ears alone, "If you're too injured to go on, you won't make the squad." I gritted my teeth and nodded. My left foot throbbed, but I could wiggle my toes.

One of the trainers tried to help me up, but I waved him off. "I got this," I said, and pulled myself to my feet. "Moutsos?" the sergeant said, striding towards me. "Fine," I said. "Fine." "Then get going," the sergeant said. "This is a timed test. Remember?" I refused to limp, despite the searing pain. I mounted my bike. The engine roared to life and I felt that roar deep in my chest. *Go, go, go,* I thought. And go I did. I burst forward and continued the course.

An hour later, foot still aching, I got my time. I'd made it. Four of us finally passed. We celebrated and congratulated one another on overcoming what for me, at least, was the hardest week of my career, mentally and physically. I went home and had to cut my boot up the side to get my swollen foot out. It was black and blue. But I'd made it. I'd made it. I was going to be a motor cop. To this day my foot is still in pain from this accident.

I awaited the official word of my transfer to the motorcycle squad, but my phone never rang. No email came. No text. Nothing. I'd heard the other three spots were instantly filled with the other three officers who'd passed. The final spot remained open.

I was at home on my day off. I paced my living room, limping slightly because of my aching left foot. *Just make the call*, I told myself. I had to know. I called one of the three sergeants over the motor squad. She answered on the fourth ring. I asked why I hadn't been called yet. The female sergeant hesitated. I waited.

Finally, she said, "I guess there was some kind of issue with you disobeying an order or something." "Really?" I said, anger leaking into my voice. "Is there anything in my file about that?" "That's the thing," she said, "you don't have anything in your file. You've never been disciplined in your six years." She paused, then resumed. "This isn't good." "No," I said, "It isn't. The truth is, sergeant, I'm betting I wasn't written up by the sergeant who's slandering me because he can't back up his claims. You know you can't just write someone up because you don't like them as an individual."

"Yes," she said. "Well, Eric, I'll make a few calls and get back to you." I thanked her and we ended our conversation. I squeezed my phone in both hands and pressed the cool plastic to my forehead, thinking this through and hoping she could do something for me. It turned out that she could and did. She called back to inform me that I had a meeting tomorrow with the chief over that department, Chief Franz.

The papers rustled in my trembling hand. My heart thumped a fretful tune inside my chest. I straightened my uniform; I made sure my boots had a quick spit shine. "Come in," Chief Franz said. I lifted my chin and strode into the office. Chief Franz watched me with a placid expression. He gestured to the chair in front of his desk. I sat. "Thank you for seeing me, sir." He nodded. I placed the papers on his desk, right-side-up from his perspective. Chief Franz arched an eyebrow. I nodded to the papers. "I pulled my stats from when I was on bike squad. Out of nineteen bicycle officers, East and West side of the city, I was consistently ranked one or two in every category for producers."

Chief Franz didn't take the papers or even look at them. I suspected he already knew. "Tell me about the conflict you had with your bicycle squad sergeant." I nodded and explained in detail how we were forced to make a specific number of misdemeanor arrests without any officer discretion. I told about my misgivings and how I'd expressed them to my sergeant at the time and how he'd reacted and forced me to stay after work without pay to meet my quota.

I said, "I can't help but be uncomfortable with such a strict quota system.Every arrest is different. Sometimes there are better solutions than doling out the maximum punishment, or forcing what someone has done into as many different crimes as possible, just to up the numbers. I seriously worry how this would look to the public, the people we're trying to serve--not upset. We want the public to see us as their friends and protectors, not as bullies just looking to squeeze out an extra buck from every confrontation."

Chief Franz looked down, his eyes searching his desk for...what? A response? I waited and, as my mouth grew drier, I wished for a glass of water. The chief returned his attention to me. "Well," he said, "you know we write traffic tickets on motors, right?" "Absolutely, sir. But I also know that a traffic ticket is different than slapping a criminal case on someone's record just because your shift is about to end and you're under pressure to get one more number before the day ends." Chief Franz nodded. He didn't look pleased, but he nodded. He said, "Anything else you'd like to say?"

I leaned forward a bit and said, "I did my job, sir. I did a great job. My numbers prove that an officer can get numbers and be motivated without the threat of unfulfilled quotas hanging over his neck like a guillotine." The chief cocked his head to the side and said, "You know, the motors training sergeant, Sergeant Weiner, told the lieutenant, who told me, that you didn't have what it takes to be good on a motorcycle. He said you were too scared on the bike." I grimaced and scrambled for an answer. *Well, why not the truth.* "He's right," I said. The chief blinked in surprise.

"But," I said, "each day I got better. My scores and times through the obstacle courses don't lie. Honestly, sir, Sergeant Weiner seems like a mostly negative guy, who doesn't come across as very, uh, affable. I don't think I heard him say much of anything positive about anyone who went through the course." Chief Franz leaned back. "Well, Officer Moutsos, I'll think about your situation and call you soon. Thank you." I stood, shook his hand, and left.

A couple of days later, I received a call from Chief Franz. Motors had picked me to fill their final vacancy. I was shocked. I was excited. I also had a deep fear that I had somehow just dug my own grave.

⸺⸻⸺

At the start of my first day on duty as a motor cop, my new sergeant sat me down in her office and outlined how things operated. "Twenty tickets," she said. My eyebrows shot up. I knew the chief said we had to write traffic tickets, just not this many per day. My old sergeant on the bicycle squad had mentioned motors had 20 tickets per day, but I thought he was exaggerating. But wow. It was real.

"I know, I know, it's quadruple what they expected on the bicycle squad, but it's completely doable. You can also get two DUI's per shift. It's a points system and you can earn X-time." I gave my head a quick shake. "X-time? I've never heard of that."

"We keep it a secret on motors, mostly," my sergeant said, and chuckled. "Anyway, one ticket equals one point. One DUI is ten points. Look, Eric, I know you've had some reservations about statistics in the past, but it's what administration wants. It's like this everywhere you'll go. Stats is how it operates. Just do what's expected of you, keep your head down, and make a good career here on motors." "Okay," I said, "so what's X-time?"

"It's personal time you'll need, especially working the afternoon shift. Busier. More DUI's are expected at night, as opposed to the day shift--but you'll need a lot more time in to get days." She snorted happily, then resumed. "You see, you'll need to get a minimum number of DUI's and you'll need time to go to court and still get those DUI's. Therefore, you need time off or you'll be forever working, either on the streets or in the courtroom. It's a perk we have as motors"

My sergeant asked a few more questions, more of a personal nature. Married or not? Kids or not? What were my hobbies, etc.? I left her office in a bit of a daze. I tried to do the math. Twenty-five motor cops writing twenty tickets per day. If the average motor cop worked two hundred days in the year...I shook my head. That was a lot of tickets. And a lot of money for the city.

I tried to reason everything in my mind. I remember thinking and somehow coming to a justification that traffic tickets weren't the same as criminal citations for misdemeanors or felonies. I had to make it right in my mind. And I really did want to get any and all drunk drivers off the streets. If there were a dozen drunk drivers on the streets in a night, I'd want to catch a dozen drunk drivers.I also never wanted to get into trouble again for not hitting numbers. There was no way out.

Well, I'd work hard. I'd do my job and keep my head down, like my sergeant advised, but I would try to not sell my soul in the process. At least not all of my soul.

CHAPTER 20

Let's Not Bring Him Up Then

It wasn't long before I felt competent in my new role as a motor cop. Riding a motorcycle felt increasingly natural, like the BMW was an extension of my body. I was familiar with the job, what to do, and when. I knew where things went. I understood what was expected of me.

Officer Campbell poked his head into our lineup room. "Hey, sarge sent a message, said something came up. She'll be a little late. I'm grabbing some coffee. Anyone else want some?" A group of officers hanging out in the back of the room raised their hands.Officer Campbell left. "So, Moutsos," one of the officers in the back said, "do you really think I'm going to hell because I drink coffee and alcohol?" I twisted around on my seat to see who'd spoken. Officer Williams, a stocky man with a bristly mustache, watched me with a poorly suppressed grin.

A couple of his friends sniggered. I said, "What are you talking about?"

"You know," Officer Williams said, "your religion teaches it's a sin to smoke and drink coffee and alcohol, right?" I groaned inwardly, but kept my expression neutral. The slight majority of the motor cops I worked with were not religious. Most were courteous, but a few of them had become increasingly rude towards my faith. I told myself it wasn't mean-spirited, more like a hazing ritual directed at the new guy. The female officer, Officer Lewis, was the worst, or at least the most blatant to my face. I remember her saying, "Hey, Moutsos, you read your golden book today?" talking about some of my church's scriptures.

I had shrugged nonchalantly and said, "Yeah, in fact I did. Just a little before work. And, it comes in vinyl...the gold ones are more expensive." "By the way," Lewis responded, "I read your Facebook posts and found them offensive." "Really?" I had said. "There's a simple fix to that you know." I opened my phone and unfriended her as she stood there staring. Officer Williams opened his mouth, but said nothing. Confusion contorted his features.

To his left, Officer Soto said, "Tell us about the secret things you do in your temples." Behind Soto, Officer Baze said, "He can't talk about that. He's sworn a blood oath." "What are you talking about?" I said. Baze shrugged. "Just something I watched on YouTube." I rolled my eyes, which got a couple of them to shake with quiet amusement. "No," Williams said, "but seriously, why do you--all of you Christians--think you get to go to heaven but everyone else goes to hell?" I started to answer, but Officer Lewis stood, shot me a hostile look, and interrupted. "You should probably pray to your Baby Jesus before you answer that."

Strong language for a home-wrecker, I thought, but was glad I didn't say it out loud--she would have scratched out my eyes. So, instead, I stared at her in annoyed disbelief as she sauntered past and out of the line-up room. I glanced at the three members of my faith sitting in the room. They just watched, squirming, looking like they wished to be anywhere but here.

The group of vocal unbelievers peppered me with questions. I answered them as politely and as thoroughly as I could. Most of them lost their air of ridicule and at least appeared to be interested in what I said. I thought it turned into a productive conversation. Our sergeant finally arrived and we got down to business.

I worked hard that afternoon. I was already halfway to my twenty tickets. There was a certain freedom that came from being on a motorcycle. I wasn't tied to my radio. I had to work hard, had to hit my numbers, but I got to choose when and how I worked. I could bust my butt for several hours, then take a break and decompress towards the end of shift if I wanted. Today, I decided to go up the nearby canyon. I wanted some time to think about the talk I'd had with my fellow officers before our lineup meeting started. I usually Monday morning quarterback those kinds of conversations, wishing I'd said this or that, but not this time. I thought I'd answered as well as I could have.

I drove up the snaking canyon road and the temperature cooled. The sun began to set, casting Salt Lake City in the colors of dusk. I thought, *It doesn't get better than this. Paid to ride a motorcycle. The wind, the hum of the engine, the motion of the bike roaring up the narrow road. The best. I'll never leave motors.* There were some great, hard-working professionals on my squad, but even if everyone was like Officer Lewis, I'd still stay. The bike made everything worth it.

I thought about the last get-together motors had. The barbecue was good, the conversations not so good. I felt like a loner pretty quickly. I'd had enough of crude conversations during my rowdy years in my late teens, before I'd realized my life wasn't what I wanted it to be, before I'd found God. It seemed like all that the majority of my coworkers wanted to talk about was women's body parts and what they'd like to do with so-and-so, their parties and who was the biggest drunk, or the negative gossiping and backbiting, especially about their ex-spouses, ex-boyfriends, or behind-the-scene girlfriends. They seemed to thrive on those topics. I didn't want to be around it. Still, I wanted to be apart of the team. Was it possible?

From high on a mountain top, I watched the city lights pop into existence, the valley becoming a vast twinkling bowl. Soon, I headed down the mountain and back to work. The next day, at the start of another shift, I strolled into our line-up room.I was about to sit when Officer Williams asked if he could have a quick second with me outside about yesterday's conversation.

"Of course," I said, and followed him out to where our bikes were. I wondered if something I'd said had reached him, touched his heart, sparked an interest in knowing more, but out of earshot of his buddies to avoid embarrassment. "Hey," Williams said, "I just want you to know, as a friend, that you upset a few of the guys on the squad for bringing up God." I blinked at him in disbelief. "You aren't serious?" Williams offered me a sympathetic smile and shrugged. I thought he was joking. He wasn't. "You're the one who brought it up," I said. "You asked me questions. I answered them."

"Well," Williams said, "the guys think you imposed your faith a little too strongly and elaborated a little too much." I shook my head and looked down. Then a thought that I'd never considered popped into my head. "Can I ask you a question?" "Sure," he said.

"Can someone be religiously into pornography?" "What?" Williams said, glancing to the left and snorting a laugh, "Are you saying I'm into porn?" "No," I said, "I'm just asking a hypothetical. Can someone be religiously into sports, or cars, or fishing, or whatever? When I say 'religiously,' I mean that's all they think and talk about?" "What are you getting at?" Williams said.

"When Christians say they worship God," I said, "what they really mean is that they put God above other things. That's what's important to them. If fishing is the most important thing to someone, then they worship fishing in the same sense that I worship God. I go to church each Sunday. A guy who loves fishing goes fishing every weekend. So, when you guys all sit in the motorcycle office and you mostly talk about sex, and women's body parts the way you do, don't you think you're imposing your religion on me?"
He scowled. "Oh, hey now, that's not the same." "Ya, it is. In fact, you say that I bring up God too much?" Nodding, Williams said, "Well, you kinda do. I mean, even if you don't say it, people on the squad know what you're thinking. They think it's weird." "So now I'm talking about religion without saying a word, because people just know what I'm thinking. What is that, telepathic preaching?" "You get what I'm saying," Williams said.

"The irony," I said, "is that you guys bring up God's name way more times than I do each day. God this and Jesus Christ that. How about this: I won't bring Him up if you don't." Williams opened his mouth, but only stared, his eyes sort of glazing over as he tried to grasp what I was saying. "If the others want me to not mention God in reverence," I said, "even though the only times I've brought Him up was when I was asked, then they, and you, can't mention His name in vain two hundred times a day. Deal?"

His eyes narrowed suspiciously. "Respect goes both ways," I said. "You want me to respect your religion, then how about you respect my religion." "I suppose," Williams said. "Just think on it," I said, and headed back to the lineup room, leaving him to mull over our conversation. As I went inside, I wondered how he would later spin this conversation to his buddies. I smiled, imagining Williams facing them, explaining how they couldn't swear anymore, and getting flustered by their bewildered expressions.

Well, I didn't really expect them to stop swearing. I could only hope that Williams understood a little better where I was coming from. And not just me. I could tell that their disrespect for others' beliefs, intentional or not, and their crude remarks, made others on the squad uncomfortable. No one should have to feel uncomfortable for their beliefs, especially at a public workplace. After all, we had a very important Amendment in the Constitution that protected us, didn't we?

CHAPTER 21

"I have a dream that my four little children will one day live in a nation where they will not be judged by the color of their skin but by the content of their character."

—MARTIN LUTHER KING, JR.

Discrimination Day

On a chilly morning in February 2014, I arrived at the Pioneer Precinct. I entered with other officers, all of us heading to one of our training rooms for our yearly diversity training, presented by the Salt Lake City Human Resources Division. I glanced at Officer McClane and said, "You think it will be worse than last year?" McClane laughed. "Is that even possible?" "I guess we'll see," I said.

We entered the training room, found seats at one of the tables, and shed our coats. About forty police officers attended. "Hey," one of my friends whispered, "we're already celebrating diversity. We have deputy chiefs here, lieutenants, detectives, and patrol officers. Very diverse. Class dismissed."

"Man," another officer said, "I hate these kinds of training." "Because it's as boring as riding shotgun in your patrol car?" someone said. An Asian woman in a gray blouse and black skirt stood at the front of the class: our instructor. She beamed and said, "Welcome to Diversity Training."

Chairs shifted and officers sat. Someone at the table behind me groaned. Silence eventually subdued the room. My coworkers stared blearily ahead, many slouching, some with heads hung, some gulping coffee or energy drinks. I felt unusually alert. Strange, because I'd even missed my caffeine in the form of a daily Dr. Pepper. "Good morning," our instructor said. "My name is Cynthia. You're cops, so my first question for today is: How do you know if an Asian robbed you?" I frowned and wondered if I'd heard her correctly. Cynthia grinned. "Your homework is done and the cat is gone."

I sat ramrod straight; my eyes shifted left, then right. Most of us were looking around at each other, as if wondering how we should respond. Should we laugh, those expressions seemed to ask, or should we be quiet, because it's obviously a trap, and we'll get in trouble if we laugh? The rest of the class hunched and busied themselves with their phones. I considered raising my hand to share a Greek joke, since my grandparents were immigrants from Greece. We could have a bad ethnic joke battle.

Cynthia continued. "What happens when you spin an Asian man on a swivel chair?" She beamed, arched a slender eyebrow, waited a beat, then said, "No one? Well, he gets 'disoriented.'" Cynthia giggled. I shook my head in disbelief. If anyone of a different race had dared to say what she just said about her own race, their heads would roll. Cynthia held up a red button in her right fist and clicked. The words projected onto the whiteboard at the front of the class switched to a pie chart. The heading said, "Demographic of People SLC utilizes as a corporation."

Cynthia clicked her red button again. There were now two pie charts, the original that represented Salt Lake City, and a second that represented the racial demographics of Salt Lake County. "You see here," Cynthia said, "a comparison of our county population compared to us as a city government. How are we doing?"
She paused, one expectant eyebrow raised. We remained silent. She continued to wait.

Finally, one of my partners on the motorcycle squad raised his hand. Cynthia smiled and pointed. "Yes. You." "Well," the officer said, "it looks like we're actually doing pretty good when you compare the county versus the city."

Everyone looked at the chart – the numbers in the department in fact mirrored an almost exact percentage snapshot of the county. Cynthia's smile wilted to a grimace. "We as Salt Lake City Corporation believe we can do a lot better."

Our instructor went on to explain how we had an unequal balance with upper management in the police department. We severely lacked minority representation.

She then related a personal story of how she was paid $10,000 less in a year than a white coworker who was performing the same job. Her lips tightened as she spoke and her scowl deepened. The ambience in the room grew increasingly uncomfortable. I thought, *Not a problem here, since a female officer is paid the same as a male officer, unless the male officer worked more overtime. Move on, please. Move on.* I fidgeted as she ranted about inequality and injustice. My heart beat a bit faster. I raised my hand. "Don't do it, Moutsos," a friend to my left whispered.

"Yes," Cynthia said, and pointed at me. "Uh, ma'am," I said, "correct me if I'm wrong, but what you seem to be saying is that if I put in an application for advancement in our department and everything looks the same on paper, compared to a, um, a minority, or a female, then, me, being white and a male, I'll be automatically passed up for the job?"

"Of course," she said without hesitation, "how else would we do it?" The room froze. My eyebrows lifted in surprise. In the past, the favoritism shown to minority groups for promotions had always been implied, never vocalized in such a straightforward manner. It was always the elephant in the room no one wanted to acknowledge. I said, "Ma'am, let me try to rephrase the question, and please correct me if I'm wrong."

To my right, someone hissed in a low voice, "Shut up, Moutsos. You'll make the class go longer." I ignored my friend and plowed forward. "If I look the same on paper as someone that's in a smaller slice in the piechart..." I held up the copy of the pie chart we'd been given in our handout."I'm not going to get the job because of the color of my skin, being white, right?" Cynthia huffed, shrugged, and said, "Again, how else are we going to do it? We want a diverse workforce."

Someone blurted, "But that's discrimination against anyone white." Not to mention the chart matched the actual numbers represented in the county. Multiple hushed, but heated conversations broke out around the room. I relaxed back against my chair and watched, surprised by the extent of the chaos my comments had spawned.

Our instructor raised her voice. She struggled to regain control. She clicked her red button and shoved her way through to the next section of the class. The projection on the whiteboard showed another chart, breaking down the current racial demographics in the population of Salt Lake City: 20%Hispanic; 4% Asian; 3% African American; 1% Native American; 2.3% LGBT. I squinted at the last part, thinking, *I didn't know LGBT was a race.*

I sighed, suddenly bored of this same old diversity indoctrination, and a little overwhelmed that we had reached a place where the reverse discrimination was actually openly owned by the employer. I slipped my phone out, checked my texts, my emails, Facebook, and tried hard to just ignore the rest of the class. Forty minutes later, the class ended. I waited until everyone left—or fled in haste--then I wandered to the front of the class, where Cynthia was stuffing items into her bag.

I cleared my throat and, when she looked up, said, "I appreciate the effort you put into this class, but ma'am, what you're teaching is extremely poisonous."Cynthia straightened, forgetting her things and giving me her full attention.I said, "Everyone in our department knows there's a problem with qualified people getting passed up for a job or promotion. Beneath the surface, there's a lot of resentment. No one appreciates politics affecting promotions."

Nodding, she said, "I understand your objections, but you have to understand that how we promote isn't designed to punish anyone, but to help those who come from a disadvantaged background. The sixties weren't that long ago. Minorities had to fight just for basic rights, rights taken for granted by a privileged white patriarchy. The mayor and the city council feel it's only right to make up for that ugly past by giving minorities a hand up."
I shook my head. "I'm very aware of what happened in the sixties and earlier in our country's history. I don't condone

the mistreatment of anyone.Racism disgusts me. But if we aren't careful, we can repeat the sixties, but in reverse. Why should anyone be discriminated against because of their skin, white or black, or anything in between?"

"Well," she said, "I'm sorry if you feel that way." "Oh," I said, "one more thing. You had LGBT listed as a race." Cynthia nodded. "But that's not a race," I said. "I do agree with you on that one," she said. "However, the mayor wants that in the presentation, and I have to teach what he wants, as handed down tome from my boss."

"Okay," I said. "Do you mind if I get your boss's name and number? I'd like to ask a few follow-up questions."Cynthia scribbled on a piece of paper, then handed it to me. The paper had a name, Sarah Brown, followed by a phone number. I thanked her, left, and followed our conversation up with an email to help her soak in the message a bit more.

I sat in my living room pondering what I should say to Cynthia's boss, Sarah Brown. My thoughts kept circling back to Deputy Chief Mountebank. A few months ago, Mountebank became the first female ever promoted to deputy chief. She was now in command of an entire bureau, the boss of lieutenants, sergeants, and officers. The press covered this progressive promotion -- such fairness, such a modern police department we had here in Salt Lake City.

The problem, in my mind, was the fact that Mountebank was not, nor ever had been, an actual police officer. The only experience she'd had with law enforcement was writing grant proposals for the Police Department. She had no police certification. She couldn't carry a gun. She was a civilian in officer's clothing.

She even had a police car issued to her with lights and sirens, which ironically, had gotten her into a bit of trouble. She'd stopped to assist an officer from another agency who was dealing with a traffic accident. Mountebank swaggered up to the officer to "assist" him. He asked who she was and where was her gun if she was a police officer? As the story went, Mountebank tried to explain, but the officer was in the middle of a high stress situation with people in need of medical assistance and traffic zipping by, creating a dangerous situation. The officer ordered her to sit in her car and stay out of the way. Had I been that officer, I probably would have suspected that she was pretending to be a cop, someone who had stolen a uniform, maybe even mentally ill.

I stood, then sat back down. I didn't know what to say or how to say it, butI knew I had to make the call. *Just do it, you idiot,* I told myself.I dialed the number. Voicemail. I left Sarah Brown a message, then did a few chores around the house, trying to keep myself occupied.

My phone rang. It was a city number I didn't recognize. My heart raced. I murmured a quick, silent prayer. "Hello," I said, "This is Eric Moutsos." "Hi Officer Moutsos, this is Sarah Brown from HR. I saw that you called.How can I help you?" "Hey, sorry," I said. "Listen, I'm a bit nervous about this. I don't want to offend anyone, but I feel like this is something that needs to be said." "Okay," Sarah said. "Well, don't worry. HR has an open-door policy. I'm here to help. What's on your mind?"

I explained the pie chart from our diversity class and how I felt that, if I ever tried to promote, I'd have an uphill battle for no other reason than because I fit into the 85% white category. I explained how Cynthia came right out and stated that if two people looked equally qualified on paper, they'd automatically go with the minority. When I finished speaking, Sarah was quiet for a moment before finally saying, "Cynthia said that?" "Yes," I said. Silence. I stood and began to pace. What was Sarah thinking?

A question occurred, striking my thoughts like a bolt of lightning. I stopped pacing. "Sarah?" I said. "Oh, uh, yes, sorry, Mr. Moutsos." "May I ask you a question? You really don't have to answer it, but I'll pose it anyway, if that's okay?" "Sure," she said slowly. "What if a fire department hired a fire chief who had never fought a fire? He had zero training in firefighting, zero hands-on experience, didn't even goto firefighting school, nothing. But the fire department hires this chief just to make them look more diverse, because he's a minority."

Sarah cut me off and with a bit of peppy indignation said, "I'll tell you right now that wouldn't happen. That's not what we mean when we talk about diversity. The person would be clearly unqualified."I smiled. "Sarah, I'm really glad you said that.""Why is that?"

"Because we have, right now, a woman deputy chief of police who is over an entire bureau of police officers and she has never been a cop. She was never trained as a cop. She doesn't carry a gun. In fact, she's been caught turning on her lights and sirens, even though she has no right to legally do so. Did you know that?"

The line went silent. She had to know who I referred to. Finally, Sarah said, "Is that all you wanted to talk about, Officer Moutsos?" "Just one thing." "Okay." "People in our police department don't dare say anything about these things because they are afraid they will get in trouble. They are afraid to speak up. They don't want to be blacklisted. They don't want to be labeled something negative." I forced a laugh. "I'm afraid myself right now, talking to you, but I believe I needed to say something." "Is that all Officer Moutsos?" "Ya, I guess that's all." Sarah hung up without another word.

That evening, as I headed to work, I replayed my conversation with Sarah. Was I wrong to say what I said? Would I have said anything different? I decided the answer was no. I'd said what needed to be said. Not long after that phone call, I was taking a break at work, having a snack and talking to my current sergeant. After the usual chit-chat about how we were doing, how our families were, and so forth, she turned serious.

"Eric," she said, "I overheard, at a command staff meeting, about your comments in diversity training." I rolled my eyes. I said, "Well, there was a chief and some lieutenants in the class. I figured my comments would ruffle some feathers." "Apparently, you also called HR." I scowled. "You heard about that?" She nodded. "I guess I'm not surprised. Our department loves to gossip." "Did you know I never originally put in for this position?" I stared at her. "Serious?"

She nodded. "The department came to me and asked me to be over motor squad. I said I wasn't interested. A week later, they asked again. I had the same response. I didn't want the position, so I'd rather be a sergeant somewhere else. Another week passed. Administration comes to me again and this time they don't ask. They tell me I will be the motor sergeant and I start Monday."

I laughed. "I've never heard of anyone being forced into a promotion." "Oh," she said, "You've never heard of being voluntold? It gets better. I showed up for training to get certified on the motorcycle. There were a suspicious number of people there, people who didn't belong to a regular training session. News crews showed up."

My eyebrows shot up. I leaned forward. "Why would there be news crews?" she said. "Well, I found out the next day when I read the headline in the news. It said, 'Salt Lake City's Motorcycle Cop Makes History!' Eric, it makes me wonder if they just used me for a headline." She leaned back on her plastic chair and wilted. "That's disgusting," I said. "Well," she said, "it gets worse." "How's that?"

She shook her head and snarled. "I'll never know if my promotion came because I was qualified or because I'm a woman. All it did was create hostility and I know some officers make fun of me behind my back, especially on the Motorcycle Squad." "You're a great sergeant," I said. "One of the best I've had; and besides, this isn't the only place this is happening." "What do you mean?" I looked up at her. "Same thing is happening in SWAT." She glanced away and down at the floor. "I won't be your sergeant for much longer."

My jaw dropped. "What? Why?" "I'm sure I'll be transferred soon. They got their headline. I'm no longer useful here and Sergeant Weiner, the guy who trained you for motors, he wants me gone. He won't stop until he gets what he wants."

I shook my head. "I'm so sorry. You don't deserve this crap." She said, "They use diversity to make themselves look good and feel good.""Who will be the new motors sergeant after you?" I said. She shrugged. "I think you'll be temporarily assigned to one of the two other sergeants until someone is selected. Maybe someone the news can do a story on."

They ended up running her out of motors just like she said they would. They used her. And that's the very reason why I spoke up. She was an incredible person who always tried to do the right thing. It's rare to find a supervisor like her. She later retired and got out of law enforcement altogether. I'm just happy she got her pension.

CHAPTER 22

Smoking Gun

At the beginning of another day at work, our lineup meeting concluded, I went to my locker to retrieve my motorcycle helmet and begin my shift. I picked up the helmet and noticed a tiny picture stuck to the back. I scowled and wondered how long it had been there. Everyone had about two inches behind their helmet to express a little individuality with a sticker of their choosing. Some attached a sports team icon, or a word, or a picture that carried significance for that officer. I had chosen a Superman sticker, which to me, represented hope.

However, this day a crudely drawn angel blowing a trumpet was swapped with my Superman symbol. I sensed someone watching and turned. Officer Lewis stood just inside the small room, smirking. I glared. She said, "What's your problem?" I shoved my helmet to another officer who was standing nearby, arms folded, grinning. "Did you do this?" I asked him. Officer Lewis laughed, a smug, nasally cackle. "That's funny. I wish I had thought of it." She sauntered past me, grabbed her gear, and left.

Near the end of May 2014, rumors began to circulate regarding who would be assigned to the annual Utah Gay Pride Parade. Usually, officers at the low end of the seniority list were assigned these duties. Given my relative newness to motors, I'd likely be assigned to the parade, which I didn't foresee as a huge problem. However, it was an overtime event and not part of my 40-hour workweek. I wasn't super keen on getting the extra time since it was on a Sunday, of all days. Between the bicycle squad and motor squad, I had probably provided security for over thirty free speech events, everything from Race for the Cure to Occupy Salt Lake, from anti-police protests to LGBT gatherings, so on and so forth.

As more details regarding the parade trickled out through the grape-vine, my suspicion was confirmed. I would indeed be assigned to ride my motorcycle in the parade. Usually, this meant providing a wedge formation at the head of the parade to clear the streets, ensuring the safety of those participating in the parade. I'd done this before. Not a huge deal.

Then more information came to light. This year would be different. Those riding motorcycles would not only clear the way for security purposes, but would be required to participate in the parade, conducting choreographed stunts for the crowd's entertainment. This revelation created an uneasy feeling in the back of my mind and on my heart. I was okay executing my police duties to protect the event, but participate in the parade? That had not been done before.

I had no problem with the LGBT community as a whole, or as individual people. In fact, I had been in the news in 2009 protecting them. "Utah Gay Kiss Police Report Sides With Couple," according to *On Top Magazine*, which told the story of how I "sided" with two men detained by Church security.

The men were slightly inebriated, kissing in public on LDS church property at Temple Square in downtown Salt Lake City. Church security had detained the two men and called police. Out of dozens of officers on duty, of course I was the one dispatched. Although technically the gay couple broke the law, I felt their actions did not amount to public intox and did not warrant taking them to jail.

In fact, I probably would have let the two men off with only a warning, but the pressure of hitting our numbers always loomed, so I cited them for trespassing as the property was, in fact, owned by the church. They were asked to leave.

I removed their handcuffs and thanked the two men for being respectful to me when I showed up on the scene. I was a member of the church, but I did not let that membership shape the way I conducted myself in my police capacity. My guide was local law and Salt Lake PD policy and procedures.

All that said, parts of the gay agenda did conflict with my religious beliefs and personal convictions. The more I learned about our role in the upcoming parade, the more uneasy I became. I discovered that the department was getting$900 for the "service." What, were we a police force for hire now? Would we be forced to do maneuvers for the Westboro Baptist Church for $900? No, how about a cool thousand? Would the department force pro-life officers to perform in a pro-abortion parade? Would the department now have to lead the KKK parade if they came marching through? How would we have a leg to stand on if we excluded one group over another? Who was to say which political causes were legitimate or not?

This was why police had to be neutral and not used as political pawns. Justice was supposed to be blind, not subjective supportive of one group over another.
I recalled that in last year's pride parade, Chief Cainam had worn the gay pride rainbow over his uniform, despite that being against uniform policy. The department had also ordered officers to hand out stickers with the pride rainbow draped over the police department badge to the kids in at-

tendance. *Yes,* I thought, *this is for real.* The rumors were true. We would be forced to participate in support of the parade.

After a few days of reflection, I decided that the easiest way out was simply to ask another officer for a trade. We did it all the time. Our squad policy was that we could trade out from two events per year, regardless of the reason.Even my own sergeant, Jackman, got out of the event that day.

On May 29, 2014, at 5:00 pm, I entered the motorcycle shed to start my shift, found the officer I was looking for, and said, "Hey, man, would you mind taking my spot at the head of the parade? I'll do your security post." I explained to him my reservation. The officer shrugged, then said, "Ya, no problem. I get it." I exhaled with relief. "Thanks, bro. I appreciate it."

I noticed Officer Lewis near the door that led inside. She was listening to our conversation and glaring at me, but didn't say anything. She spun and walked back inside. *Whatever,* I thought. *The trade has already been made.* I felt a weight lift from my shoulders. I smiled and headed for my motorcycle. About an hour later, an email came down the chain of command from the motor Sergeant Weiner regarding the Gay Pride event. At the bottom of the email, it stated:

"...Unfortunately, no bumping or trading...will be permitted. This has only been permitted in the past when having a pre-approved excusal from the event itself."

Why now, after 100 years of policy, was this order issued? I had never seen an email like it. Why would he send an email saying "No trading", if he didn't already know a trade had been in place? He wouldn't have. This was the smoking gun, and the reasoning was transparent. They wanted to force me to go against my beliefs, and perhaps others like me, into doing what they wanted. For their agenda. For their secular irreligion. I bowed my head, shoulders sagging, and sighed heavily.

Well, I thought, *I guess I'm in the parade.* Except I wouldn't be in the parade. A few days before the event, I wouldn't even have my badge. I would never work for the Salt Lake City Police Department again.

Part of my official email back to the Sergeant a week before the parade happened.

XXXXX,

"I have no uneasy feelings working any other assignment on this day at the event; security, parade post, traffic, etc. I do take issue about doing maneuvers; because it looks like we (and I) are in support. I don't think it's a good idea they use our police agency to do this. I would have these same feelings if, and even though it's legal, about being in an abortion parade, etc; I would feel extremely uncomfortable being a spectacle and would ask that you please allow me the choice for someone to trade me for whatever reason, if at all possible....

To be clear as well, I do not hate gay people. I love them like I love humanity. I just disagree with this particular movement, like I do abortion...There is a giant difference between working a traffic post as police and being in a parade on display. Especially if the officer has the choice to switch someone."

Officer Moutsos

CHAPTER 23

"Hope is being able to see that there is light despite all of the darkness."
—DESMOND TUTU

Hope Through Heartache

Administrative leave. I still couldn't believe this was real and not some waking nightmare. It certainly felt surreal. Sergeant Jackman left my home. He took my spare badge. He took all the city's property that I had in my possession. It felt like he took my identity. I didn't know who I was. Stacey kept asking questions that I couldn't even process. I didn't have answers anyway. Stacey was crying. I was crying. "Let's go to your rooms," Stacey told the kids. "Why?" Devery said. "What's happening?" "Why are you and Daddy crying?" Ava asked. Stacey forced a smile. "It's okay. Now go to your rooms."

My youngest stared at me with big, wet eyes that pleaded, feared, and floundered. I saw my own emotions in those eyes. Maybe that's why I felt so empty inside. "Daddy," Devery said, "do we have to go?" "It's okay, honey," Stacey

said with a crack in her voice, "just go ahead and go up."
Daddy, I thought. *Yes, I am still a dad. I'm just not a police officer at the moment.* What would Dad do to feed these children? A good dad feeds his children. A good dad has a job. How can Dad feed his children now?

I turned back to the window and watched my former sergeant drive away with all my dreams. Would he ever bring those dreams back? I thought, *Deputy Chief Franz and Lieutenant Ewing will realize they're wrong. They'll call me tomorrow and apologize for the misunderstanding. Then I'll remember who I was.* What was pressing against my chest? I glanced down and there was nothing there. Why was it so hard to fill my lungs? My throat burned and my cheeks were wet.

"Stacey," I said, so quiet I almost couldn't hear myself. "Oh, Stacey. I'm sorry. I'm so sorry." They took my identity, but my heart was still here, in this home, with my family. I squeezed my burning eyes shut. A few hours later, I placed the sleeping pill on my tongue and thought, *This isn't a sleeping pill; it's a waking pill. I'll wake up from this nightmare after I take it.* Stacey offered our prayers because I couldn't quite frame a coherent thought. I rolled into bed. Stacey kissed my unresponsive lips. The lights went out. In the darkness, I could feel her concerned gaze against the side of my face.

I stared at the ceiling. The ceiling stared back, never blinking.I jerked awake. I snapped upright. I blinked. Was I dreaming? My heart pounded. Was that a heart attack? No. Not that. But my chest. I couldn't breathe right. Stacey slept. I snuck out of bed. I went to the office, the computer, and to the internet.I researched how to breathe. Breathing exercises. Calming inhalations. Slow exhalations. They didn't work. Back to bed. Stared at the ceiling. Fell asleep. Woke up startled. It wasn't a dream. Breathe. Fail to breathe. Exhausted. Stared at the ceiling. Fell asleep.

Woke up startled. Breathe... I just wanted to sleep and not wake up. Morning imposed its will upon my life. Still not dreaming. I didn't know what to do, so I sat on my couch. The house was silent. Stacey took the kids to buy a few groceries.

I wasn't a union member, so I couldn't turn to them for help. The last two union presidents were puppets on Chief Cainam' strings and the most recent president was terminated for allegedly stealing thousands of dollars from the union. So why join? What would be the point? I also wasn't a member of the Fraternal Order of Police, in part because it cost $30 per month and I never imagined I'd be in a predicament like this. No, not me. I could spend that $30 a hundred other places.

The wheel of time creaked and groaned and trudged around and around. Day. Night. It didn't matter. I'd sleep at noon and blink at the wall at midnight. I stopped eating. Food revolted me. I couldn't force a slice of bread down. It was all I could do to even move.

***

June 6th, my dad and brother yanked me out of bed. "Come on, son, we're going golfing." I stared at my father and he glared back. I nodded once. I dressed and we headed outside. It was very bright and very hot. Was this the first time I'd been outside since...when? Had I really never left the house since my badge was taken?

At the golf course, I attempted a few swings before giving up. I just watched my dad and brother play. My brother bought me my favorite drink Dr. Pepper. But it tasted too sweet and the carbonation burned my throat. I tried to force smiling. I burped up foam and dumped the rest of the soda on the grass. *I'm breaking apart,* I thought. *Little bits of me, I leave them behind, everywhere I go. I have to figure out what to do about this.*

Several holes later, my phone buzzed. A text message from my brother-in- law: Eric, you have to read this." I clicked on the attached link. It took me to the Salt Lake Tribune website. The heading of the article was: "Utah Police Officer on Leave for Refusing Gay Pride Parade Assignment." From the article, I read: *A Salt Lake City police officer has been put on leave due to allegations that he refused to work at this weekend's Utah Pride Parade. "If you refuse to do an assignment, that's going to be a problem inside the police department," police spokeswoman said Friday of the need for officers to follow orders. Internal affairs officers are investigating the officer's refusal while he is on paid leave, she confirmed.*

She would not discuss the officer's reason for refusing the assignment, but said: "The vast majority of officers, when they come to work, they understand that they leave their personal beliefs at home and serve the community."

The article didn't name the officer. I thought to myself, *Oh, someone else on the squad said something, too.* After too many moments, my eyes widened. I mouthed the word, "No." They were talking about me. But how could they be? I didn't refuse to work the parade. I just didn't want to be *in* the parade.

My knees struck the grass. I wobbled to my feet and crawled onto the back of the golf cart. The world blurred. My throat burned. My abdominals convulsed.
My father and brother noticed my sobs. I couldn't see them, but I felt their hands and heard their voices. "What?" my dad kept saying. "What?" After a struggle to compose myself, I showed them the article. We left the golf course. Within only a few hours, the story went national. It eventually reached other countries. With every retelling of my sto-

ry, I thought, *That isn't true. I didn't refuse. I tried to trade spots with another officer, something within policy, something that happened in almost every event that we provided security. They're lying on purpose.*

Later, at home, slumped on my living room couch, I watched our Public Information officer, Linda Stone, on the evening news giving a statement. She said the officer refused a post. Lie. She had to know what was really happening.She had to know the officer simply asked for a trade out of being part of the celebration.

She said, "When officers come to work they keep their personal beliefs at home
and provide service to the community... "We do not tolerate bias, bigotry, within the organization." Other people interviewed. Assumptions made based on inaccurate information. "Clearly, the officer chose to act in a bigoted way," Greg Nguyen of the Utah Pride Center said.

Personal beliefs, I thought. *If I have to leave my personal beliefs at home why is an entire police department celebrating someone's sexual beliefs? We protect everyone. We don't pick sides. But the chief chose sides, didn't he? I just wasn't on his side. Do I have to accept someone's sexual beliefs to love them or protect them as people? If I'm threatened to accept something I don't believe, then who is the target of prejudice?*

The next report that hit world news was from our Salt Lake County District Attorney. He was wearing the rainbow colors over his neck as he spoke on public TV. He said that I should, "be in a different profession." Who had the DA talked to? For sure not me. Why was he commenting on my case? Tipping the scales of justice? All of these thoughts raced through my mind.

"It's over," I said aloud. That night, I didn't sleep. My mind couldn't shut down. It's hard to sleep when you are the target of negative national and world news. So I spent the dark hours of night devouring the even darker comments people posted after the articles. Anonymity and no fear of confrontation or reprisal made men and women bold. People called me names, called for public beatings, wished me suffering and grotesque modes of death. Some were positive, even thought-provoking, but such posts were outnumbered.

As I read comment after filthy comment, I started to feel something again. Not anger at the angry, but determination. I had to make a decision about all this and about my life. But what? Black thoughts assaulted my mind, a sinister voice, almost a presence, that screamed that I should give up. It was as if I heard an audible voice, "Where is your God now?"

The next morning, I tried to get out of bed, but physically couldn't. The lack of food was taking a serious toll. At thirty-three years old, I had been in the best shape of my life. I'd gone to the gym for years, building strength, building size, building my body. It would take only weeks to undo what I'd spent years building. I'd gone from 180 pounds to 158 pounds. I was starting to look like I'd never lifted a weight in my life.

Stacey struggled not to weep as she rubbed my legs. She helped me sit up and massaged my back. My wife, my best friend. Stacey left our bedroom to make me some toast. I lay on my side and pulled into a fetal position. I stared at the knob of a dresser drawer. I wanted to melt away. *Pray.* The word rested gently inside my head. *Pray.* I gritted my teeth. *Pray.* I heaved my body, twisted and wriggled, then slid off the side of the bed. I knelt, leaning against the side of the bed for support. "God," I said in a raspy voice that I barely recognized. "God, please, I need help. Please help me."

I sat on the floor, leaning against the bed. Moments later, my phone rang. The sound terrified me. I trembled. It could be one of the people who hated me, one of the people from the posted comments lurking beneath news articles. *Answer it.* I blinked. Yes, I had to answer it. I grabbed my phone from the nightstand. I didn't recognize the number. What if it was...? *Answer it.* I answered, but said nothing, just listened, tense and uncertain. "Hello?" a male voice said. I swallowed, trying to work up enough moisture in my mouth to speak. "Who is this?" I said. "My name is Rhett Branson.

I am an attorney here in Utah. I heard what happened. We are going to help you."

I didn't know who this person was, but I felt a flicker of light inside me during our brief conversation. I knew that God had sent him to me. Stacey and my parents accompanied me to the law office in Sandy, Utah, to meet with Branson. It was a Saturday. Branson arranged to meet with us privately in his conference room over the weekend. We sat on large chairs at a large table. I started telling Branson my story, not just my cop story, but everything, my whole life just tumbling out of my mouth. My youth. My family. My music. Evander Holyfield and his record label. My beliefs about God. All of it.

Branson sat there, watching me, never interrupting. I stopped talking. I felt exhausted, like the end of a marathon. Branson exhaled. He pursed his lips, then said, "Dude, why are you a cop?" He shook his head. "You don't seem like a cop." I glanced uncertainly at Stacey, then back to Branson. The attorney said, "What do you want to do with the Salt Lake City Police Department?"

I shook my head and stared at the bottle of water on the table before me. Deep down, in my gut, I knew my career with the city was over. If I fought them for one reason, then they'd attack me from another angle. If I fought that angle, they'd find another, then another. That's the way it worked. Especially in Government. Once you were on their radar, it was over. Even if I got my job back, it would be a hostile working environment. I'd never advance within the department - like a motor cop looking for a traffic violation...they'd eventually find it. They'd even broken their own policy about not commenting on an ongoing internal investigation. That showed their commitment. I knew that I had only one course of action.

"I have to resign," I said. Branson looked at me. "No, you don't. I can think of a dozen ways to come at these guys, and they deserve it for this one." I nodded. Branson said, "You can go after them under Title VII of the Civil Rights Act of 1964. The city is in blatant violation. They should have accommodated your trade." "I want to resign," I said. "But I also want people to know the truth." Branson sighed, then nodded. "Okay. But you can do both. You don't have to decide today, but you have a case without question." I hesitated. I thought about the men and women I served with. I thought about the police academy and about the role and mission of policing. I thought about the people I served.

"I don't want to take anything from these people." Branson folded his arms and sat back in the leather chair. "They are probably insured. You're not necessarily taking anything from them." "I don't know," I said. "It feels dark to me." "We send in your resignation. We draw up a letter, a press release. We send that to the media, how you never refused any assignment, and you have the emails to prove it, and that the department violated its own policies by not doing a

proper investigation before commenting on your case."
"Yes," I said, "that sounds right. That feels right." Branson
paused, studied me a moment, then said, "Eric, you want to
know something interesting?" I shrugged.

Branson continued, "About ten months ago, there was a
certain deputy chief over internal affairs placed on administrative leave. Why? Well, for allegedly sexually harassing
three women at work. The deputy chief was accused of shar-
ing private, sexually suggestive images of a female officer,
and another image of two other female officers in bikinis.
The women complained." "Okay," I said, frowning. "I know
the case. What does that have to do with me?"

Branson looked sternly at me. "Isn't it interesting that the
investigation took ten months? Ten...long...months. Interesting that the investigation concluded just after the deputy
chief hit his twenty years with the city so he could retire
with his pension. City administration gives this guy, who
should be fired, ten months, when they run others out of the
department in a matter of weeks, and for less. Well, you
should know that this story came out in the media the same
day that your story came out. Thirty minutes before your
story came out, to be exact. You see where I'm going with
this?"

I stared at Branson, while the implications started to form
in my mind."Eric," Branson said, "how do you get rid of a
scandal in the news?" My eyes widened. Branson grinned.

"That's right. You bring out a bigger scandal. Everyone forgets about the shady actions of a police department dragging out a sexual harassment investigation for ten months to protect their buddy by using you to run interference. Besides, from what you've told me, it seems they were dying for a reason to get rid of you." "Is that true?" Stacey said.

Branson raised his hands, shrugged, and said, "Well, who can say? The sexual harassment scandal was spreading quickly in the news then...Bam! Bigot officer hates gay people. Newsflash! It was the perfect storm for them - get rid of you and cover up the rest of it at the same time."

We sat in silence, digesting Branson's theory. Finally, he said, "You sure you don't want to go after the city in a lawsuit?" I pondered that for several minutes. I pictured the drawn out legal battle. The cost. The toll on me and on my family. I didn't want revenge. I just wanted this to end and move on.

I did, however, want the truth out there. People had to know the truth. I had to clear my name. "Okay," Branson said. "We send in a letter and the press release – whether you resign or not, you're being constructively terminated. They may clear you for this, but they'll never let up on you. In my opinion, your days in the Salt Lake City Police Department are numbered whether you try to stay on or not.What you have to decide is whether you want to use the tool of litigation to make them pay for it."

I did not revel in the thought of a litigation, but I wanted to find a way to tell my story. I wanted people to know what is happening. I shook Rhett Branson's hand and thanked him. I felt like he'd given mean other chance at life. Relief washed over me as I left the office. I felt lighter. I felt a little hope. *Finally,* I thought, *it's going to be over. I can move on.* But it wasn't that simple. Life is rarely that simple.

CHAPTER 24

"We are now entering a period of incredible ironies...we shall see in our time a maximum if indirect effort made to establish irreligion as the state religion. Irreligion as the state religion would be the worst of all combinations. Its orthodoxy would be insistent and its inquisitors inevitable. Its paid ministry would be numerous beyond belief. Its Caesars would be insufferably condescending. Its majorities—when faced with clear alternatives—would make the Barabbas choice, as did a mob centuries ago when Pilate confronted them with the need to decide."

—NEAL A. MAXWELL- MEETING THE CHALLENGES OF TODAY-
1978

Breaking Silence and Finding Peace

After my resignation, my problems were not all magically solved in a moment of wand waving. My story did not go away as I'd hoped. My side of events, despite the media now having it, was never told. Perhaps the untrue narrative, the scandalous, hateful officer story, was too juicy to give up. Perhaps the fabricated story fit someone's agenda a little too well. Either way, the national and international media were taking their turn evaluating incomplete facts.

Although my name had not yet been released publicly, everyone I knew realized that the male officer who had resigned must be me. Even some of my distant family members disbelieved my side of the story when told. Some of my cousins stopped talking to me. Many close friends deleted me from their social media. I got it. I understood. They had to be thinking, *Why would the police department lie?* Representatives of law enforcement stood on the steps of a building dedicated to truth, justice, and the enforcement of order, and called me a bigot. It must be so.

And so I hid. I hid and I worried that today was the day that the investigative journalist released my name. My bills, like my anxiety, remained a constant issue. I needed money. I found odd jobs. I mowed lawns. I painted. I approached my church for help with food. Never in my life did I think I'd ever need church welfare to make ends meet. I thought, *If I don't find a regular, full-time job soon, I'll wind up at the very homeless shelter I once patrolled.*

Court subpoenas plagued me. I was no longer an officer, but I still had to go to court to testify on all the arrests I'd made. Usually, twice each week, court proceedings swallowed my day. They paid me a paltry $18.50. Not $18.50 per hour. No, $18.50 for the entire day. I was not an officer, so I was not paid as an officer while at court. I called the city prosecutor's office to let them know I was in a hardship, scrambling to provide for my family, and this consumed my time, preventing me from focusing on full-time employment. They didn't care. One prosecutor over the phone said, "I'm sorry, it's the law. You must show up."

So I did, because I feared I would go to jail if I refused a summons. I received over seventy subpoenas to my home address, delivered by constables. Every time the doorbell rang, my heart pounded its familiar ode to anxiety. During one court case in Salt Lake City, the defense attorney said, "Are you the officer who was involved in not wanting to be in the Pride Parade?" Sitting on the stand, I recoiled in shock and horror. "Objection," the prosecutor said. "This has absolutely nothing to do with a DUI."

The defense attorney said, "And isn't it true, Mr. Moutsos, that your faith doesn't believe in drinking alcohol?" I glanced sideways at the judge, thinking that he would somehow save me from these questions. The judge looked and said, "Answer the questions."

They forced me to defend my religious faith in court regarding what I believed to be the pitfalls of alcohol. I said, "I believe people have the right to drink, but don't have the right to drive drunk, just like your client was that night."

Despite the difficulties of our new life, there were tender mercies and literal angels, seen and unseen, helping our family. That summer, our air conditioner broke. We didn't have the money to fix it, so someone paid to have it fixed. No notice, no warning...just paid and had it done. More credit card debt accrued. But from time to time, we'd get an anonymous letter with small increments of cash. God was with us.

That same, sweltering week before the A/C was fixed, we were nose-to-nose with our portable fans by day, and sleeping atop our beds at night, sweating, when our family dog of over a decade died. "I'm sorry, kids, we have to have Ramen noodles for dinner again." "I'm sorry, kids..." Despite the increasing financial difficulty, there were ongoing moments of obvious grace, moments when I knew God was looking out for us. We experienced one small miracle after another. Just enough to keep me--us--going.

I received a letter from Colorado. I didn't recognize the name at first, or address. The letter said:

Eric,

I am so sorry for what has been happening. I have experienced a similar situation and want you to know God is on your side. Don't lose hope.

Sincerely,

Jack Phillips
(Masterpiece Cakeshop)

In the envelope was $500 in cash. My legs buckled. I knelt, weeping and thanking God for this man's kindness. Jack Phillips was the man who'd been in the news for offering to sell anything in his shop to a gay couple, but refusing to make them a personalized wedding cake on the grounds that he did not want to feel like his art was being used in something he disagreed with. His case went to the Supreme Court.

Jack had not wanted to participate in a gay wedding. Elements of the government wanted to force him. I had not wanted to participate in a gay pride parade. Elements of the government wanted to force me. I called Jack and thanked him. We promised to stay in touch.

Christmas approached and we put up the lights and decorations. We managed to buy each of our children one gift. The space beneath our tree appeared so empty compared to years past.

One day, my eldest daughter, Ava, handed me something. A dollar. She said, "Here, Dad, I want you to have it." I knelt and embraced my selfless daughter. I struggled to suppress my tears.

On an evening in mid-December, someone knocked at the front door.I peeked out the window, relieved to find that it wasn't a constable with yet another subpoena. I didn't recognize the guy, so I opened the door slowly, cautiously. "Are you Eric?" He reached his right arm behind him. I tensed. My heart galloped. Was he reaching for a weapon? People had made disparaging, even violent remarks in the comments online. I positioned my right foot back in a fighting stance and made fists, ready to let loose and defend myself and my family. Time slowed. I leaned forward. His hands came up. My hands came up. He held out a shiny, red card.

The man said, "A few of my friends heard about what happened to you and wanted to give you this for Christmas." I stared at the card. I blinked at the man's face. He smiled. "Who are you?" I said. "I'm Dan Olsen." We shook hands. "Where are you from?" I asked. Dan shrugged. "Canada, actually." I flinched. "Canada?" "Merry Christmas," he said, returned to his car, and drove away. I took the card upstairs and told Stacey what happened. I opened the card and found $800.   Stacey and I stared at each other with wide eyes and mouths dropping open. "Canada?" she said. "Dan from Canada," I said.

We didn't know what else to do, so we said a prayer, thanking God for the kindness of a man named Dan from Canada. On December 23, 2014, we arrived home from dinner at my parents' house. As we pulled into the driveway, our headlights illuminated three or four shiny, colorful boxes, all gift-wrapped and each the size of various large appliances. The boxes blocked the front door.

The kids leapt out of the car, screaming and laughing. I jumped out, too, and we all dashed to the front porch. I stared in awe and glanced at Stacey. Her mouth hung open and her eyes glistened. I dragged the boxes inside. The boxes held smaller boxes. A lot of boxes.A hundred presents. I couldn't speak. Each present had a name. Our names.We'd never had a Christmas like this. We never discovered who had done this amazing kindness to us. If you happen to be reading this, thank you.

Not long after that memorable Christmas, I heard a radio broadcast from my church's officials. They were calling for legislation to balance the rights for religious freedom and also for the LGBT community.

"We urgently need laws that protect faith, communities, and individuals against discrimination and retaliation for claiming the core rights of free expression and religious practice that are at the heart of our identity as a nation and our legacy as citizens," the church spokesman said. "We must find ways to show respect for others whose beliefs, values, and behaviors differ from our own while never being forced to deny or abandon our own beliefs, values, and behaviors in the process...Every citizen's rights are best guarded when each person and group guards for others those rights they wish guarded for themselves."

Later in the news, I learned that the Utah legislature was trying to craft a bill for their next session that would deal with balancing religious freedom and gay rights. When I had heard the broadcast from my church, I began to feel a clarity that I had not experienced before. Maybe the purpose behind my trial was beginning to emerge. Now, some LGBT activists were trying to convince lawmakers that a religious freedom bill was not necessary. No need for discussion. No religious rights to conscience were being violated. There was not a single case of religious bigotry. Only gay people needed protection.

I clenched my teeth. *No,* I thought, *there's at least one person harmed for voicing their beliefs, and there will be many, many others.* What about all the people who have silently endured without saying a word? I knew I had to tell my side of what happened, though the idea terrified me. Things were just beginning to die down in the media regarding my story and my name still hadn't been officially revealed.

I got a new job in law enforcement in a smaller department. The sheriff had hired me because, as he put it, "God told me to." He was, and is, a great man. But he soon retired, declining to run for reelection. Difficulties with the new job arose. My anxiety was almost too much to handle. I began to wonder if I wanted to be a cop anymore, anywhere. Plus, as great as it was to have a job again, it never quite paid the bills in the smaller department. It was around a twenty-percent pay decrease to go to that new agency. In the end, we just couldn't do it. Plus, I still had some things I needed to say, and I imagined it would be safer to say them as a civilian.

Stacey and I discussed the idea of leaving law enforcement for good. We agreed that it might have consequences, but it was the right thing to do. This law they were discussing, and others like it, would affect us, and our children, and their children. What kind of world did we want for them?

I called a few friends, asking who in the media I should approach. Around the end of February, we had an interview lined up. The night before I was scheduled to speak to the media and reveal my identity, I said a prayer. I explained to God that I had made a choice to tell my story and that I was going to give my name to the world, come what may.

"God, please let me know if this is the right choice. I absolutely need to know." I went to sleep with confidence that I would get an answer. Somehow.

In my dream that night, I was at complete peace, something I had not felt in a very long time. Everything in the dream was so bright, so vivid, a world of greater color and intensity than the one I knew. I ascended up a verdant hill. Hundreds of families dotted the landscape, all gathered together in individual family circles, sitting on the grass. At the pinnacle, I saw the brightest, most beautiful building I had ever seen. I couldn't begin to describe the glowing whiteness. I couldn't quite tell if I was walking or floating towards that structure, but the closer I came, the stronger the feelings of peace and love. Each of the families stood as I neared, then passed them. One by one, they thanked me for what I was doing.

I awoke at 3:30 in the morning. I smiled blissfully and slipped back into a peaceful, restive sleep. I knew, in my heart, the dream had been God's answer. I thought I would be afraid during the interview, but I wasn't. I felt a confidence that wasn't normal for me. I sat in my chair and my heart beat normally. I didn't have a script. I didn't try to think of what to say. I would speak truthfully and from my heart.

The reporter began. She asked her questions. My mind felt sharp, faster than normal. After the interview, I knew I had done the right thing.

_Over the next few days, media outlets from Los Angeles to Washington, and many in between, contacted me. Surprisingly, even many super liberal outlets, like Salon Magazine, came out with articles that sided with me.

People from all over the country filled my Facebook with brief notes of gratitude and support. I wept as I read each thank you. Only two out of the hundreds of messages received were negative towards me. Two! I left law enforcement. I found other work. Not long after the interview, several Utah lawmakers contacted me, requesting that I testify at the Legislature. I sat before state representatives. I answered their questions. I felt that this was exactly where I was supposed to be at this time in my life, something that I rarely experienced.

I met a man named Jeremy Lund. Jeremy was a man suing the State of Utah to try and legalize gay marriage. As we talked, I quickly realized he seemed to be different from many of the activists who believed the way he did. He was extremely down to earth, not the angry, closed-minded radical I'd met on other occasions. He was sympathetic to my story. We exchanged numbers and he followed up with me, asking how I was doing, something I found remarkable in light of our differing opinions.

Our exchanges gave me some hope that we could all differ in our opinions and manner of thinking while still respecting one another. Months later, I received an invitation to Jeremy's wedding. Yes, a gay wedding. After much thought and prayer, I responded by thanking him for thinking of me. I explained everything about my stance on gay weddings, which he surely knew already. I told him that I didn't believe in what he was doing. However, after careful consideration, I would go to support him as a friend, as long as I wasn't in the ceremony itself. He replied that, despite knowing how I felt, he would love to have me there, supporting him as a person, while disagreeing with the act.

I asked my wife if she would go with me to the wedding, but she had a prior commitment. I wondered who I could take. It hit me. I knew the perfect person. I grabbed my phone. "Hello," my daughter's dance teacher said in a flamboyant voice. "Who's this?" "Randy," I said. "Eric?" "Yes, Randy, hey, I was invited to a gay wedding and I need a date. You want in?" "Oh, ya, baby. That sounds crazy fun." I nodded. "Okay. I'll pick you up at 2:00." "Great." "Hey, Randy..." "Hmm?" "You better look good." He laughed. I chuckled.

At the wedding, I wondered what I'd gotten myself into. I felt horribly out of place, but I still felt like attending was the right thing to do. It turned out to be a nice day with incredible food. Randy seemed to have the time of his life. I was glad he came with me. So, I watched a friend get married in an order I didn't believe in, but I still had love for him as a human being. Now what? During the ceremony, I thought about what I'd do if I had a child like Jeremy who also wanted a gay wedding. I would attend, but I would tell my child the same thing I told Jeremy. It helped me see clearer.

I reflected on my marriage to Stacey. We are members of The Church of Jesus Christ of Latter-Day Saints. We were married in our Holy Temple. We said our vows inside that sacred building, believing that what we did--marriage--was holy and ordained of God and lasts forever. When, as a married couple, we exited the temple, a diverse group greeted us.

There were many members of our family, extended family, and friends, who did not believe that our marriage meant what we believed it meant. They didn't believe our marriage was eternal. They didn't believe it would continue into the afterlife. They believed only in "'til death do us part." In fact, some believed what we were doing was a total lie. But they believed in us. I felt that this was what I had done in going to Jeremy's wedding.

That following June, Salt Lake City Police Chief Cainam was forced to resign over the way he'd handled the sexual harassment scandal from last year, among many other things. I wish I could say that I didn't smile like the Grinch who stole Christmas, but I did. *Poetic justice,* I thought. Almost exactly one year from the day that Chief Cainam condemned me, took my badge, and forced my resignation, the same was done to him. In fact, I heard after they took his badge that he tried to get into the building and his key fob didn't work. Apparently, he had a huge fit and screamed at everyone. I heard several people laughed who watched it happen. And just like that, the machine ate its oldest living child.

That same month, I received a call from my old motorcycle sergeant, Jackman, the one who dropped me off at my house and collected my city equipment. "I'm in charge of the Gay

Pride Parade this year," he said on the phone. "Okay," I said. "I wanted you to know that the LGBT group wanted the police to do celebration maneuvers and circles in the parade again." "And?" I said, "Why are you telling me this?"

"Well, when the order came down, I called my lieutenant. I told him that I received his order, but, because of that religious freedom bill that was passed, I would have to ask the guys if they wanted to do the maneuvers or not." "What did the lieutenant say?" "He couldn't say anything," Jackman said. "It's the law now. Anyway, you should know that all five officers didn't want to celebrate in the parade. Just had to call to tell you that." I paused, unsure what to feel, what to say. Vindication? Triumph? I simply, but sincerely, said, "Thanks." I hung up the phone and a small smile tugged at the corners of my mouth.

Epilogue- Final Thoughts

Recently while flying back out to Evander Holyfield's house, I sit watching the clouds from the small window of the 747. America, I think. What an incredible blessing to be living in America in this day and age.

A few hundred years ago, before the settlers of Jamestown arrived, some of the most advanced tools were little more than a shovel and a pick-axe. Now, because of the freedom that was created by a divinely inspired Constitution, I soar across the country in a jet, thousands of miles in a matter of hours.

The Founders helped build that freedom. Individual creation and invention. Anything we can think of, really, we do it. We have advanced in ways that even the most forward-thinking science fiction writers of the 19th Century could not have predicted. However, we have lost much. In the last few years, it seems we've gone back 50 years somehow.

The machine is what needs to be fixed. It's not police officers that are the problem. It's the policies and culture that are the problem. Many politicians desperately want us to be divided on false premises. I don't believe it's racism that runs rampant in these police agencies, but the fuel of quotaism sure seems to produce more problems than it solves. Nobody is talking about that. We are more alike and united than we think as Americans, but this machine needs to be repaired.

I stare ahead at the seat in front of me and wonder how my life has come to the place it has. It's almost like God is just leading me along the whole way, like the whole thing was planned from the beginning. Thinking about law enforcement now feels like a dream from years ago. Like another lifetime. Like it didn't happen.

Being able to stand on Utah's Capitol and have my story used to help pass stronger laws for religious freedom felt like a step in the right direction, but ultimately how can the Government help us to love one another? It's like each law that gets passed just drives bigger wedges between people.

I was also asked by Utah lawmakers to come and tell my story about police quotas on Capitol Hill. While testifying, there sat behind me around fifteen Utah police chiefs and their representatives to try and discourage lawmakers to not pass the bill. Some of them testified that they don't have police quotas, but were against the bill. Why would anyone be against the bill to ban police quotas if they didn't have quotas to begin with?

The Salt Lake City Police Department then came out to the media and said I wasn't telling the truth. The only problem for them, was that I brought an audio recording of my former Sergeant talking about the quotas. I played the audio for the committee. The department went silent after that. Weeks later, one of my friends at the police department sent me a screenshot of a new policy change in the department: "No recording supervisors without their knowledge." Even though state law permits. Interesting. You would think the new policy would say "No forcing officers to arrest people based on a quota system."

In April of 2018, the Utah State Auditor then performed a limited performance audit on the Salt Lake Police department regarding religious freedom and my case. They saw all the back and forth emails. In short, the audit said "SLCPD management do not fully understand the protections of religious accommodation as required by Title VII." I was interviewed by Fox News about the audit.

Earlier, in some crazy twist of fate, I had the opportunity to connect Evander Holyfield with Mitt Romney, which led to a charity boxing match between the two. It raised over a million dollars for blindness. What if I went through what I went through just to save someone's vision? Who knows?

Looking back at my life, I can now see why certain people entered in and out when they did and why. I just wish I could see what this looks like for my children. When I was a cop, I was going to have a pension. I had security. Now I have uncertainty. Where does God want me? I know I was supposed to put my story in book form, but for what? Will it help someone, somehow?

I get off the plane and meet up with the Champ, Evander Holyfield at the Hardrock Cafe. We talk for hours about life. A lot of spirituality. We aren't the same denomination, but both of us know God is in control and has our backs. Evander has been a mentor to me for over 13 years now and we've stayed in touch over the years. I even went to his 50th birthday party.

The following morning, I have the opportunity of a lifetime. I'm working out on a cardio machine, the legendary Evander Holyfield on one side, and Riddick Bowe on the other. Two Heavyweight Champions that exchanged the belt between them. They are playfully arguing who would whip each other's tail in a rematch.

We then step into a boxing ring at the back of the gym. We start shadow boxing each other. My head is down. Evander says, "Keep your head up when you're fighting, Eric. You gotta pick your punches." Those words again. They resonate deep in my soul. They have become a guiding principle in my life.

Earlier in the year, when I was with Evander, we stopped at a bistro by the beach. A small band was playing some old rock and roll songs. The group Evander and I were with demanded that I sing some Johnny Cash with the band. Folsom Prison Blues. I got up on stage and let it all out. I remembered that bar in Salt Lake City. Another lifetime ago. I sang and it felt good.

Writing this memoir has also felt good. It's been therapeutic in many ways. It's helped me realize that I don't regret what happened. The tough times made me tougher, but they also somehow made me softer. The opposition was the greatest thing for me. What we go through in life, if we let it, makes us better in ways we can't always see. But God sees. He sees how we need to be shaped, so that we, too, see a little clearer. We see better how to love. We see better what we need, what our families need, and what our communities need. If we let it, life will help us see what the world needs, and what we need to do to make it all a better place. Hopefully, this memoir helps you see a little clearer, love a little more, and follow the dictates of your conscience at the same time.

With love,

Eric Moutsos

Please connect with me at www.ericmoutsos.com for updates, news, blog, and what I'm up to today.

Thanks for going through this experience with me. I hope it helped somehow.

Eric Moutsos Letter to Salt Lake City Human Resources

Note: This letter was sent 4 months prior to losing my badge and gun for discrimination.

From: "Moutsos, Eric" <Eric.Moutsos@slcgov.com>
Date: February 11, 2014 at 6:45:06 PM MST

XXXXXXX,

I hope you didn't feel that I was challenging you as a person with my problem with the material. To me, what needs to change in the world is how a certain race (in the case we talked about happened to be a white person) will be passed for a job or promotion just to equalize the pie chart. I understand what you were saying when you asked the question "what if both people were the exact same on paper, how else could we hire, to fix the problem?" But there has got to be a better way that to look at race and sex to "balance it out".

I don't think it's a problem to have the demographics match to the state. I think it would be a problem to all involved, by artificially placing people in positions they are not qualified for; just to try and make the pie chart "even". It can and never will be even, because we all have different talents to bring to the table; and a lot happen to be mixed races.

It naturally creates two problems-

First, race, gender, sexual orientation, etc, shouldn't even be brought up during any type of hiring or promotion process. It will automatically discriminate against the person who belongs to the larger category (if two people are the exact same on paper), so the pie chart needs to be "equalized", whether that be white for the larger category, or the second category of Hispanic, etc, all the way down the line. With this thinking, someone will always be discriminated on. True diversity celebration is not trying to change the demographics of the culture, but celebrating the culture itself; what we do have.

The second problem it creates is that it's not fair to a woman or minority in the long run. It may seem like a temporary "fix" but it's a slippery slope. I'll explain.. We as human beings all have a sense of self worth inside. We all want to earn what we get and get what we earn; there's power in this. However, when someone is promoted or hired just because of their race, etc, that self worth goes out the window; and self empowerment is lost. We wouldn't feel like we actually got the job off our own merits. Likewise, it creates a hostile work environment with other employees that go for the positions. I've actually talked to a woman in our organization that feels the same way I just described. She has been promoted and doesn't know if it's because of her own merits, or because of the manipulation of the process. Think how she must feel deep inside.

The solution-

We hire based on character and competence and not gender, race, sexual orientation, etc. I know that you said there's a lot of politics behind this material and you don't agree with some of it; but something needs to be changed. The irony is this philosophy is doing the exact thing that was happening in the 60's, except opposite colors.

I would love to talk to you more how to cultivate a different approach in this thinking; to see if there's a better and healthier way for the future. Let me know and I'm thrilled you liked the book. That's the kind of material that should be on the forefront of any training. Treating people like we want to be treated.

Eric Moutsos

"You cannot have a legal right to a moral wrong." Abraham Lincoln

---

Of Interest

- http://www.freetobelieve.com/eric-moutsos
- https://www.ksl.com/?nid=148&sid=2627030
- https://www.deseretnews.com/article/705367649/Rave-at-Salt-Palace-results-in-nearly-a-dozen-arrests.html
- https://www.ksl.com/?sid=13748328
- https://www.deseretnews.com/article/865634148/Salt-Lake-police-foundations-under-FBI-investigation.html
- http://archive.sltrib.com/article.php?id=2244180&itype=CMSID
- https://www.ksl.com/?sid=21468452
- http://www.ontopmag.com/article/4196/Utah_-Gay_Kiss_Police_Report_Sides_With_Couple
- https://www.deseretnews.com/article/865604722/Salt-Lake-deputy-police-chief-accused-of-sexual-harassment-resigns.html
- http://www.foxnews.com/us/2015/06/12/salt-lake-city-police-chief-resigns-over-sexual-harassment-issue.html
- https://www.youtube.com/watch?v=7DI9SFl-LZ9Y
- https://www.deseretnews.com/article/865636116/3-officers-file-sex-harassment-law-

suit-against-ex-deputy-chief-ex-chief-Salt-Lake-City.html

- http://archive.sltrib.com/story.php?ref=/sltrib/news/58036918-78/jones-officer-police-officer-s.html.csp
- https://www.youtube.com/watch?v=gYGOm-c8zwpY
- https://www.eeoc.gov/eeoc/newsroom/wysk/workplace_religious_accommodation.cfm
- http://fox13now.com/2014/06/08/d-a-on-salt-lake-cop-who-refused-pride-parade-assignment-maybe-he-should-be-in-a-different-profession/
- https://www.ksl.com/index.php?sid=30208919&nid=481
- https://www.deseretnews.com/article/865604667/Officer-placed-on-leave-for-refusing-Utah-Pride-Parade-assignment.html
- http://www.foxnews.com/us/2014/06/07/police-officer-refuses-to-work-at-gay-pride-parade-in-utah.html
- https://www.youtube.com/watch?v=gYGOm-c8zwpY
- http://www.latimes.com/nation/la-na-utah-officer-gay-pride-20150226-story.html
- http://www.latimes.com/nation/la-na-utah-lgbt-20150306-story.html
- http://www.nydailynews.com/news/national/ex-cop-punished-objecting-pride-parade-article-1.2131375

- http://www.washingtontimes.com/news/2014/jun/9/officer-leave-after-refusing-work-gay-parade-we-do/
- https://www.salon.com/2015/02/26/should_a_cop_be_made_to_participate_in_a_gay_pride_parade/
- http://www.dailymail.co.uk/news/article-2652538/Salt-Lake-City-police-officer-forced-leave-refusing-work-gay-pride-parade-department-does-not-tolerate-bigotry.html
- http://www.theamericanconservative.com/dreher/the-prophetic-eric-moutsos
- https://www.lgbtqnation.com/2015/02/cop-who-objected-to-riding-in-gay-pride-says-he-was-unfairly-branded-a-bigot/
- http://www.breitbart.com/big-government/2016/06/15/double-standard-gays-salt-lake-city-police-force/
- http://archive.sltrib.com/article.php?id=2552820&itype=CMSID
- http://www.jamaicaobserver.com/news/Cop-refuses-to-work-at-gay-pride-parade-in-Utah
- https://www.nbcnews.com/news/us-news/mitt-romney-fights-evander-holyfield-salt-lake-city-charity-n359546
- https://www.bmi.com/news/entry/20050817_eric_ryan_joins_bmi

- https://www.bmi.com/news/entry/20050413evan-der_holyfield_boxing_champ_evander_holy-field_brings_real_dea

Deputy police chief viewed, shared sexually suggestive images

Case closed ▪ ██████ who retired Friday, was being investigated for harassment.

First Published Jun 06 2014 01:29 pm
Last Updated Jun 06 2014 09:21 pm

Utah police officer on leave for refusing Gay Pride Parade assignment

SLC police » Officer who expressed "personal opinion" is investigated by internal affairs.

First Published Jun 06 2014 01:48 pm • Last Updated Jun 07 2014 04:29 pm

On May 29, 2014, at 6:01 PM, ████████████████████ ██slcgov.com> wrote:

OK...

For starters, ███ you are out, ████ you will be the 2014 Commander!

Secondly, you **will need to** conduct *basic* Parade Maneuvers for this Event. I was under the impression we would not be doing so this year; however, I was mistaken.

In addition to ████, the following *will* comprise the Wedgie Team:

1. ████████
2. ████████
3. Moutsos
4. ████████

The determination as to who comprises the Wedgie Team is, *as always*, based on Squad Seniority. These will be your assignments for the Parade; this event is staffed as a Motor All which equates to the fact that we all have individual assignments. These assignments have already been planned out; unfortunately, no bumping or trading into or out of the Wedgie role will be permitted. This has only been permitted in the past when having a pre-approved excusal form the Event itself.

Made in the USA
Las Vegas, NV
07 July 2021